Essential Music Theory

1-3

Mark Sarnecki

San Marco Publications

Essential Music Theory © 2023 by San Marco Publications All rights reserved.

All right reserved. No part of this book may be reproduced in any form or by electronic or mechanical means including Information storage and retrieval systems without permission in writing from the author.

ISNB: 1-896499-36-8

Contents

Lesson 1: **Pitch and Notation**   1

Lesson 2: **Note Values**   17

Lesson 3: **Rests**   25

Lesson 4: **Meter**   30

Lesson 5: **Accidentals**   57

Lesson 6: **Intervals 1**   71

Lesson 7: **Major Scales**   75

Lesson 8: **Minor Scales**   93

Lesson 9: **Intervals 2**   109

Lesson 10: **Chords**   118

Lesson 11: **Melody**   132

Lesson 12: **Music Analysis**   146

History   158

Music Terms and Signs   175

This volume covers Levels 1 to 3 of Essential Music Theory. The abbreviations for these levels are ❶, ❷, and ❸ and they appear in the left margin of the page. These symbols indicate the level of the material being covered. The number ❶ refers to Level 1; the number ❷ refers to Level 2; and the number ❸ refers to Level 3. Level 1 material is required for the Level 2; Level 1 and 2 material is required for Level 3.

1
Pitch and Notation

❶❷❸ Sound - Good Vibrations!

Music is **sound**. Sound is all over the place, and you have two fantastic devices that let you hear it: your ears! Sound is created by a vibrating object, like a string, a drum head, a column of air, or a metal or wooden bar. These vibrations are sent to the ear as sound waves.

The ear is a complicated thing. The external or fleshy outer ear is called the ***pinna*** or ***auricle*** and acts like a funnel to bring sounds into your inner ear. The inner ear is called the ***cochlea*** and is a small curled tube filled with fluid that takes sound vibrations or sound waves and creates signals through nerve impulses that the brain interprets as sound. You turn on the music, the vibrations go into your ears, your brain decodes them, and you hear your favorite song.

Figure 1.1

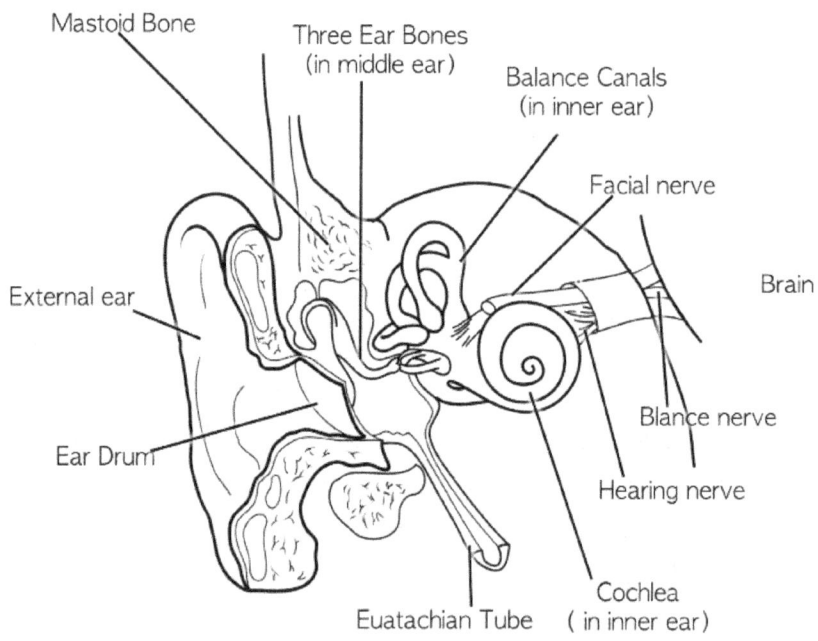

Pitch and Intensity

With the ability to hear it is not surprising that humans started to create and organize sounds into patterns that became music.

Sounds can be heard as high or low. This is called *pitch*. The faster an object like a string vibrates, the higher the pitch, the slower it vibrates, the lower the pitch. On a keyboard the higher pitched sounds are on the right and the lower pitched sounds are on the left (Figure 1.2). Understanding the keyboard when studying music theory is helpful.

Figure 1.2

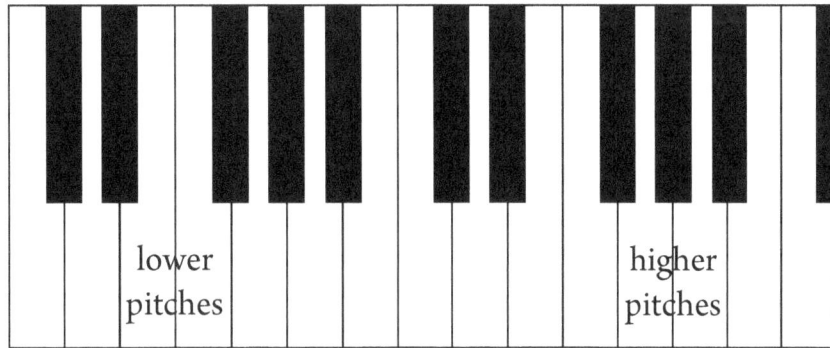

As well as pitch, music occurs in different degrees of loudness or softness. This is called *intensity*. Intensity is determined by how much power is sent to the ear by the sound wave. If you play a really loud chord on the piano with all your strength, a powerful wave is sent to your ear, and the sound intensity is loud.

Pitch may also be defined as the name of the note that you play on your instrument. The system that we use to identify different pitches is achieved by placing notes on a set of lines or spaces called the *staff*.

The Staff

Sound and music have been with us since the beginning of time. Like our languages, it was around a long time before it was written down. Originally it was taught by rote, which means it was learned by listening to it and copying what was played or sung. There was no notation. People just copied the sounds they heard.

Music has been written down for about 1000 years. This isn't very long in terms of world history. Around the year 500 AD we see the first examples of written western music. Monks in the monasteries of the Catholic church developed a system of writing notes called **neumes** (pronounced noomes). Neumes were small markings that were written above the words of a song that indicated the pitch of a note and how long to hold it. Eventually, neumes were placed on a system of lines. The line indicated a specific pitch. If the neume was above the line the pitch was higher, if the neume was below the line, the pitch was lower.

Over the years composers experimented with different ways of writing music, and around the year 1500 they came up with the system we still use today.

Figure 1.3 shows an early manuscript written with neumes.

Figure 1.3

The staff we use today is an outstanding invention. It is the home for music notes and consists of five lines with four spaces between them. The lines and spaces are numbered from the bottom up. As we study theory, we will learn that most things in music are counted from the bottom up (staff lines, notes in a scale, intervals). Figure 1.4 is a diagram of the staff lines and spaces.

Figure 1.4

```
Line 5 ─────────────────────────
                                 Space 4
Line 4 ─────────────────────────
                                 Space 3
Line 3 ─────────────────────────
                                 Space 2
Line 2 ─────────────────────────
                                 Space 1
Line 1 ─────────────────────────
```

❶❷❸ The Musical Alphabet

Every note we play has a name. Music uses a system of seven letter names to identify pitches. They are:

A B C D E F G

There are no H's, W's or Z's. After G, the musical alphabet moves back to A. On the keyboard this can be found on the white keys. Figure 1.5 shows the musical alphabet on the keyboard.

The keyboard is a great visual aid when studying music theory. The way it is laid out helps us understand nearly all of the concepts we will study in this book.

Figure 1.5

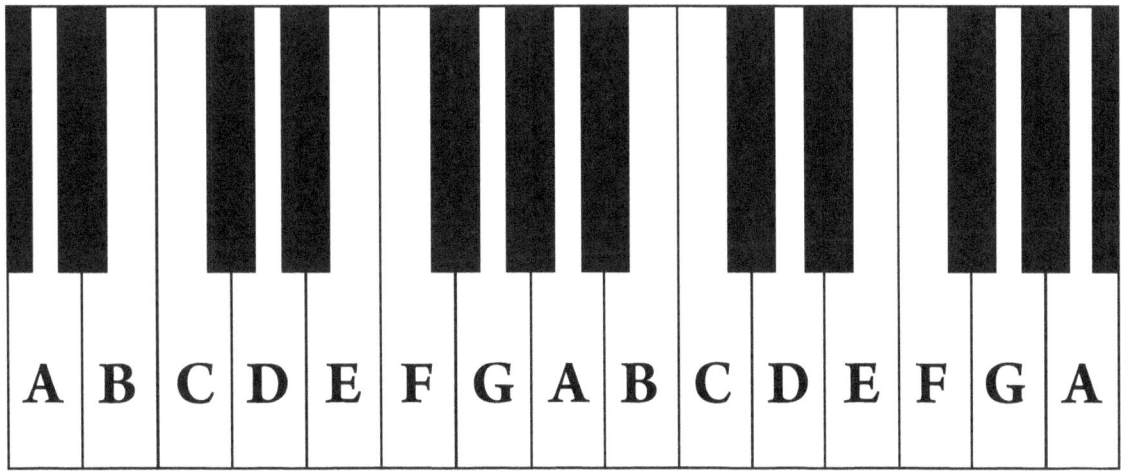

1. Number the lines and spaces on the staff.

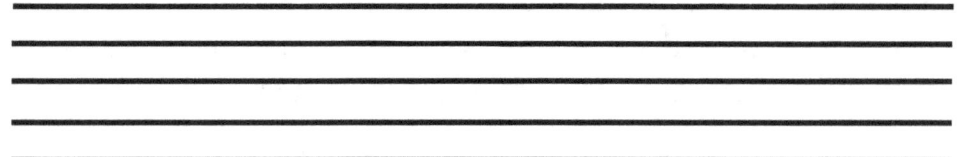

2. Write the musical alphabet on the keyboard.

The Treble Staff

We know that the staff consists of five lines and four spaces, but how do we know where the notes are on the staff? To determine this, we need a symbol called a *clef* at the beginning of the staff. The clef defines where notes go on the staff, like a map.

The *treble clef* is the most common clef. It looks a little like a fancy letter G. The inner loop of the treble clef circles around the second line of the staff. The second line is where the note G is located. For this reason, the treble clef is sometimes called the *G clef*.

Figure 1.6

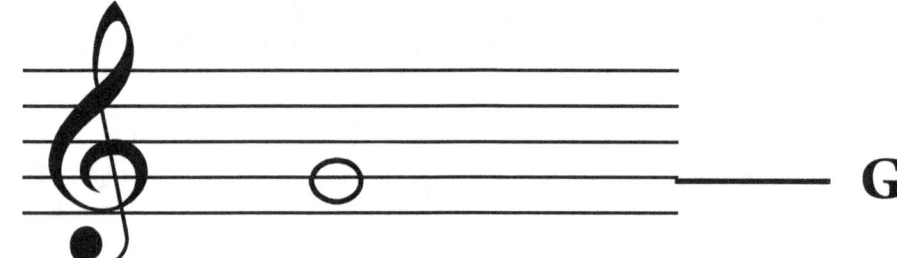

Pitch and Notation

3. Draw several treble clefs in a row.

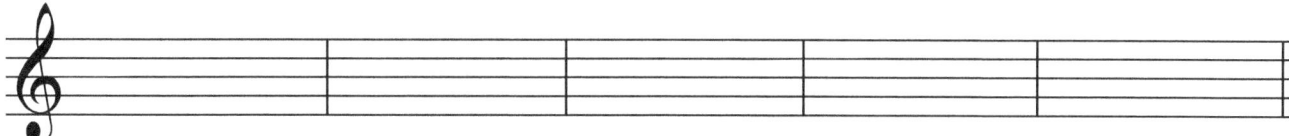

The treble clef is used by instruments with a higher pitch like the flute, guitar, violin, trumpet, clarinet, saxophone and piano.

Space Notes

A space note is a note that occurs within the spaces of the staff. They are placed between the lines without crossing over the lines. When we refer to space notes we say they are **in** a space. For example, in Figure 1.7, the first note is **in** the second space.

Figure 1.7

Line Notes

A line note has a line going through its middle. When drawing a line note be sure that the line goes directly through the middle of the note. Line notes are said to be **on** a line. In Figure 1.8, the first note is **on** line 3.

Figure 1.8

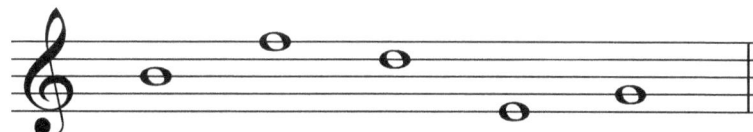

❶ Knowing that G occurs on the second line of the treble staff, using the musical alphabet, it is easy
❷ to fill in the remaining notes of the treble staff.
❸

Figure 1.9

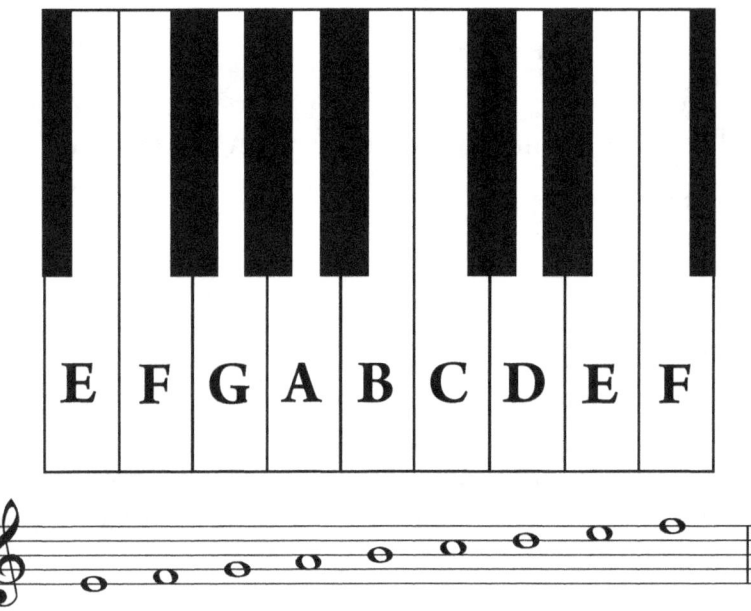

A *mnemonic device* is a great way to help you remember the notes on the treble staff. Mnemonic comes from the Greek word to remember. There are many sayings to help you remember note names.

Figure 1.10 is a saying for the line notes. Can you make up your own? Be careful when you draw a line note. The line must go right through the middle of the note.

Figure 1.10

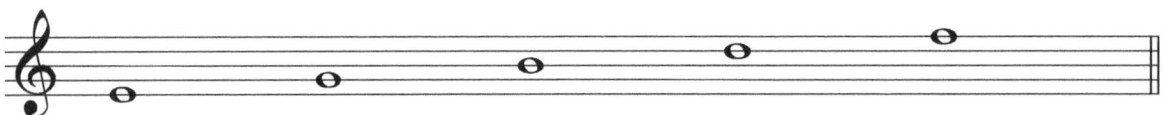

Every   Good   Burger   Deserves   Fries

The space notes of the treble clef spell the word FACE. When drawing a space note keep it in the middle of the space and try not to go over the lines.

Figure 1.11

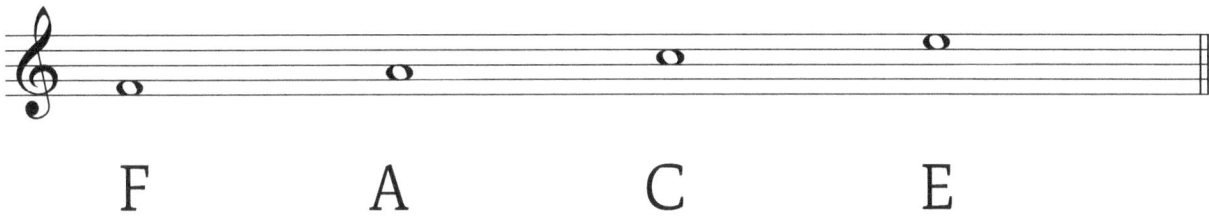

1. Name the following notes.

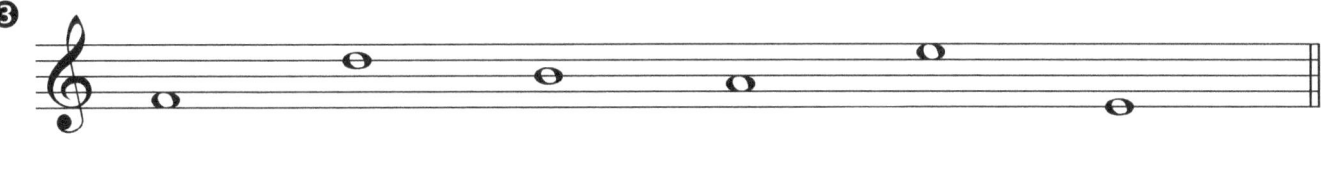

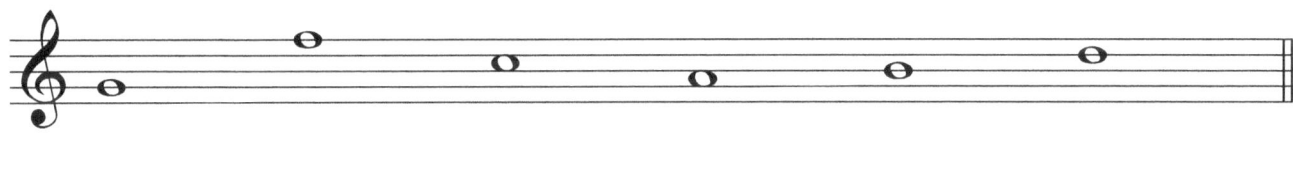

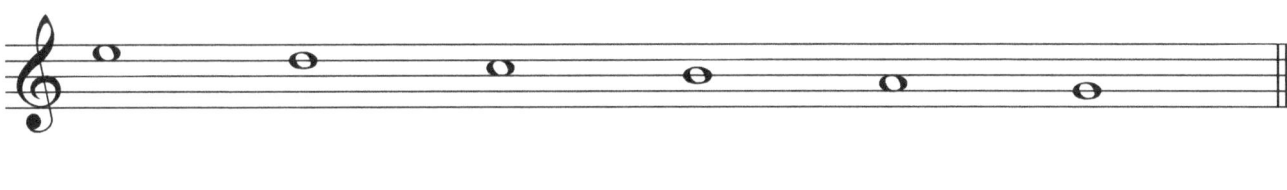

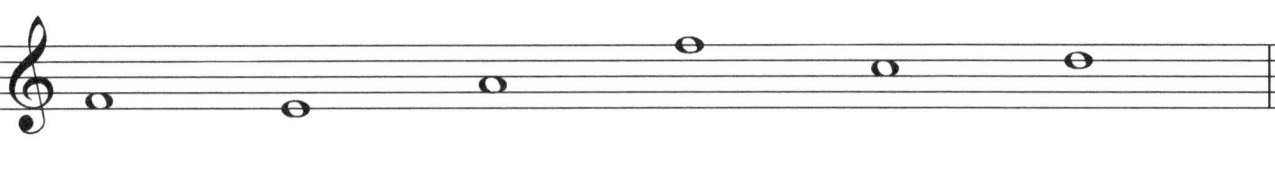

The Bass Staff

The ***bass staff*** uses the ***bass clef*** (pronounced: base) and covers the lower sounds in music. The bass clef is sometimes called the F clef because it looks like a fancy F and it has two dots that surround the fourth line which holds the note F.

Figure 1.12

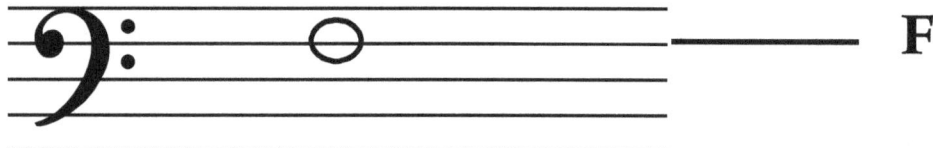

1. Draw several bass clefs in a row.

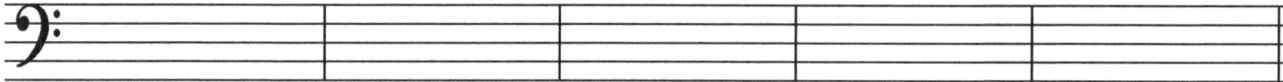

Many lower pitched instruments use the bass clef like the tuba, string bass, cello, trombone, and piano.
Since we know where F is on the bass staff, it is easy to find the other notes.

Figure 1.13

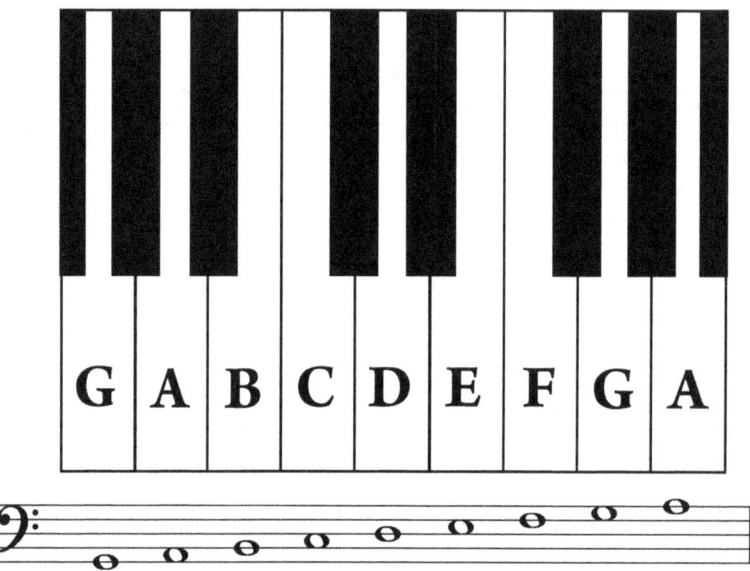

© San Marco Publications 2023 — Pitch and Notation

An easy way to remember the notes on the bass staff is to use the sayings in Figure 1.14.

Figure 1.14

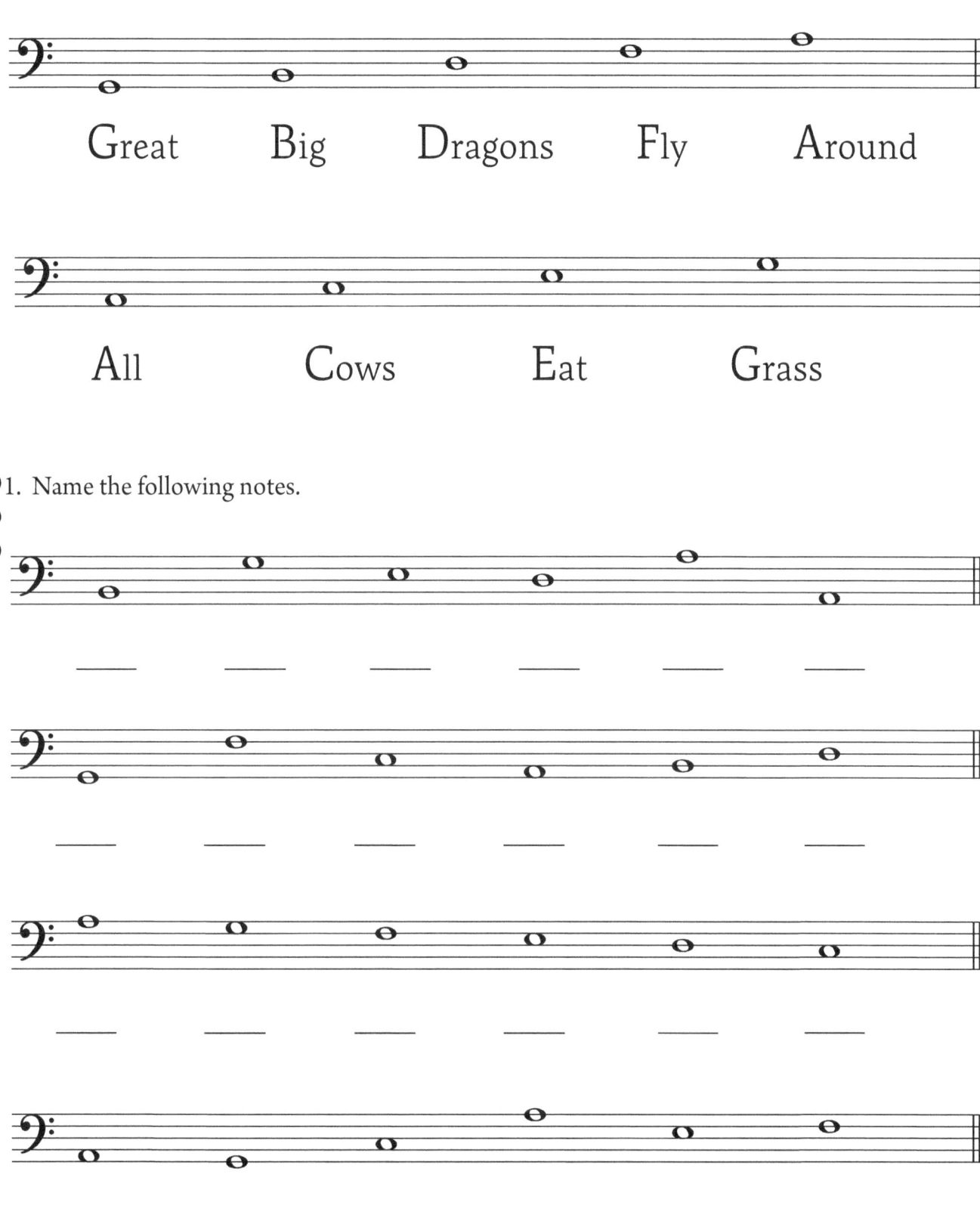

1. Name the following notes.

Ledger Lines - Extending the Staff

A staff has five lines and four spaces and holds nine notes. However, there are a lot more than nine notes. A staff can be extended up and down using small lines called **ledger lines**. A ledger line is a small horizontal line spaced the same distance as the lines of the staff itself. It occurs above or below, and holds the notes that are higher or lower than the staff. A ledger line is only as long as the note it is attached to, and is never used unless it is attached to a note. The alphabetical order of the musical alphabet continues as you move above or below the staff using ledger lines. In this level, we are going to study notes that are three ledger lines above and below the staff. Figure 1.2 shows the notes that are three ledger lines above and below the treble staff.

Figure 1.2

Figure 1.3 shows the notes that are three ledger lines above and below the bass staff.

Figure 1.3

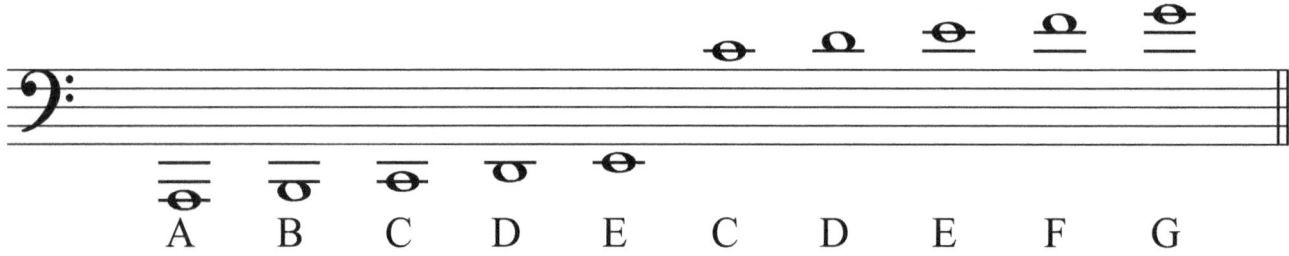

1. Name the following notes.

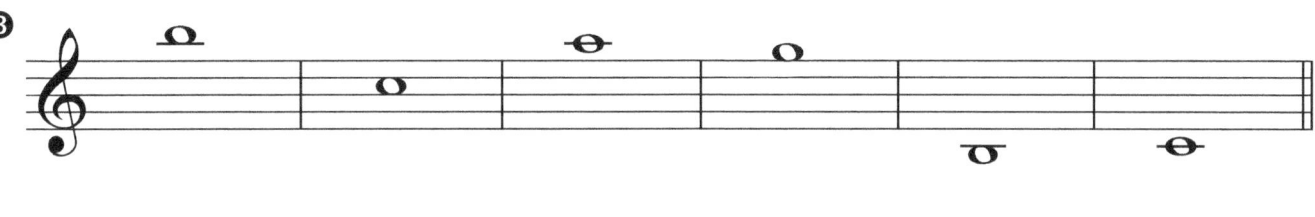

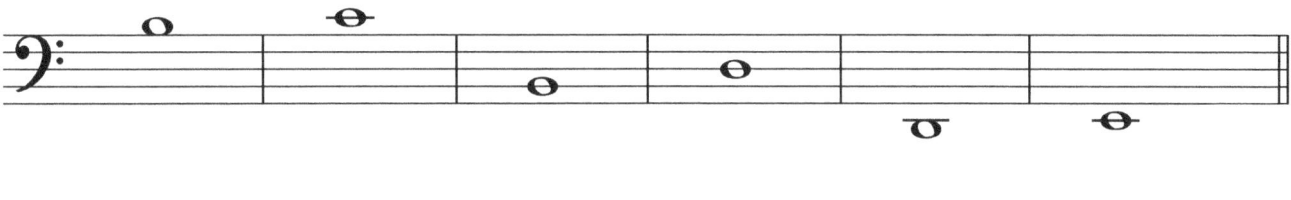

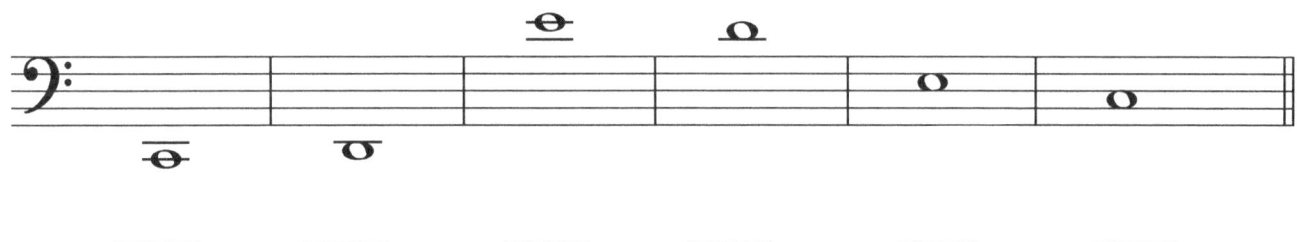

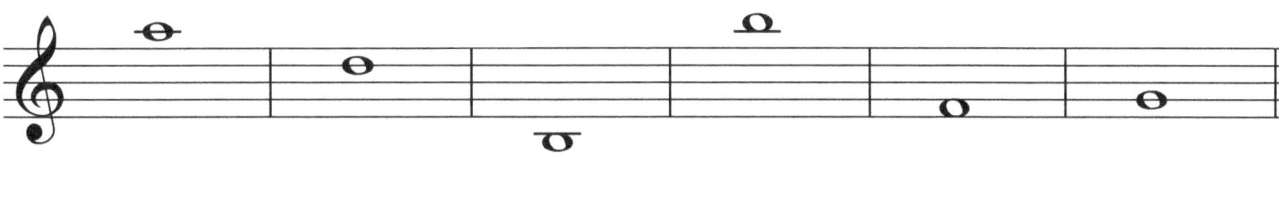

❶ 2. Write the following notes using ledger lines below the treble staff.
❷
❸

        A   C   B   C   B   A

3. Write the following notes using ledger lines above the treble staff.

        A   B   C   A   C   B

4. Write the following notes using ledger lines below the bass staff.

        C   D   E   D   C   E

5. Write the following notes using ledger lines above the bass staff.

        D   C   E   D   E   C

6. Write the following notes anywhere on the staff.

        A   G   E   F   D   C

        B   A   G   D   F   E

The Grand Staff

When you combine the treble and bass staves, you get the *grand staff*. This staff is used by the piano because both clefs are needed to cover its extensive range. The treble clef is on the top and the bass clef is on the bottom. They are joined by a line and a brace or bracket. Figure 1.17 contains the grand staff with its notes. Notice that middle C occurs in both clefs in the middle of the grand staff.

Figure 1.17

1. Name the following notes on the grand staff.

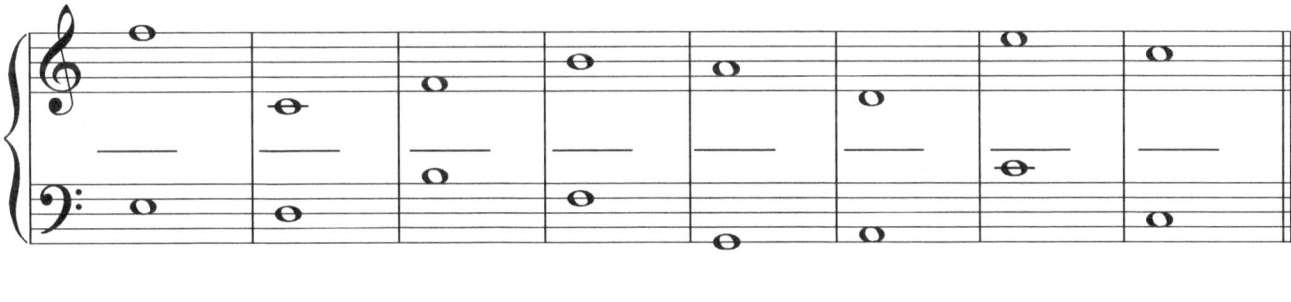

2. Write the following notes on the grand staff.

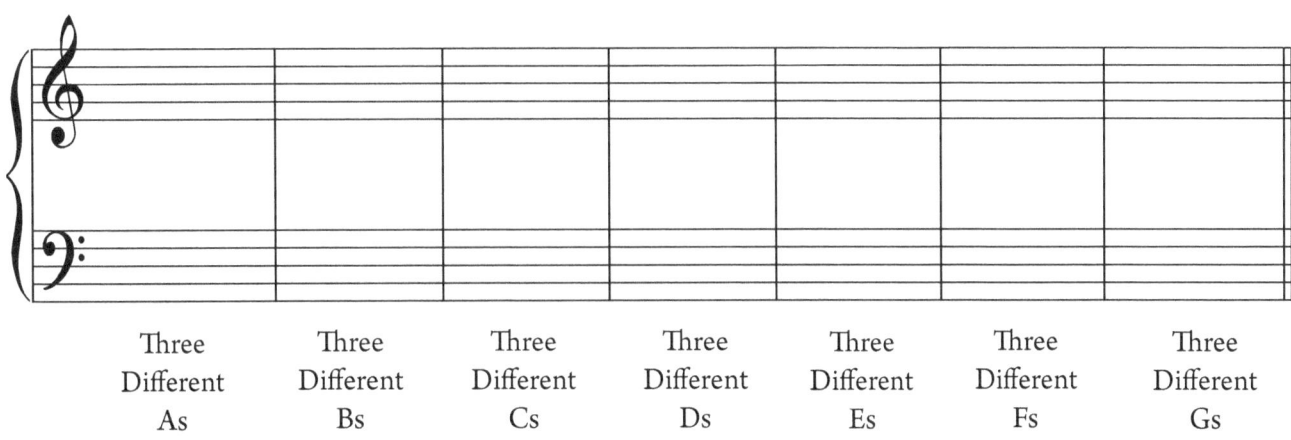

Three Different As, Three Different Bs, Three Different Cs, Three Different Ds, Three Different Es, Three Different Fs, Three Different Gs

❶
❷ 3. Name the notes and draw lines matching them with the keyboard.
❸

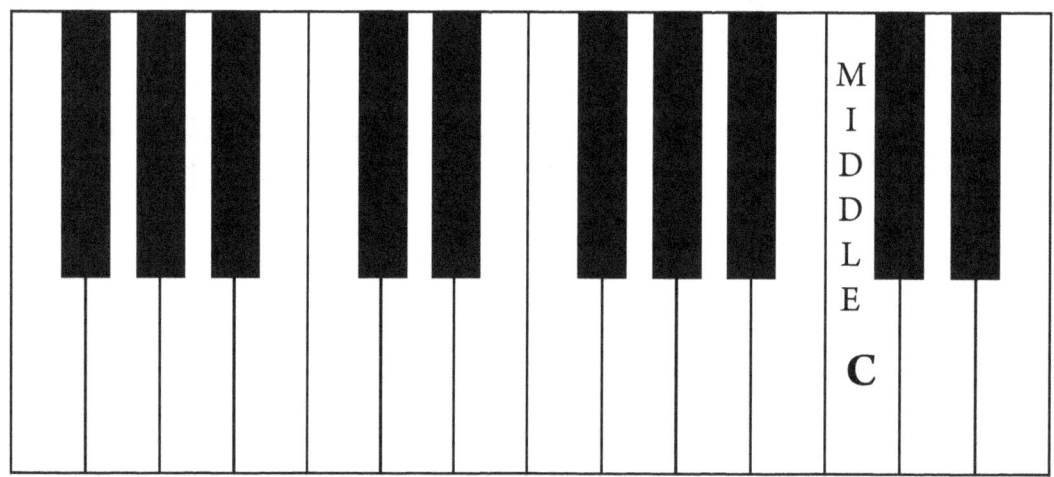

Pitch and Notation

Word Exchange

Name the following space notes which spell words. Write them again in the blank measures using only notes that are on **lines**.

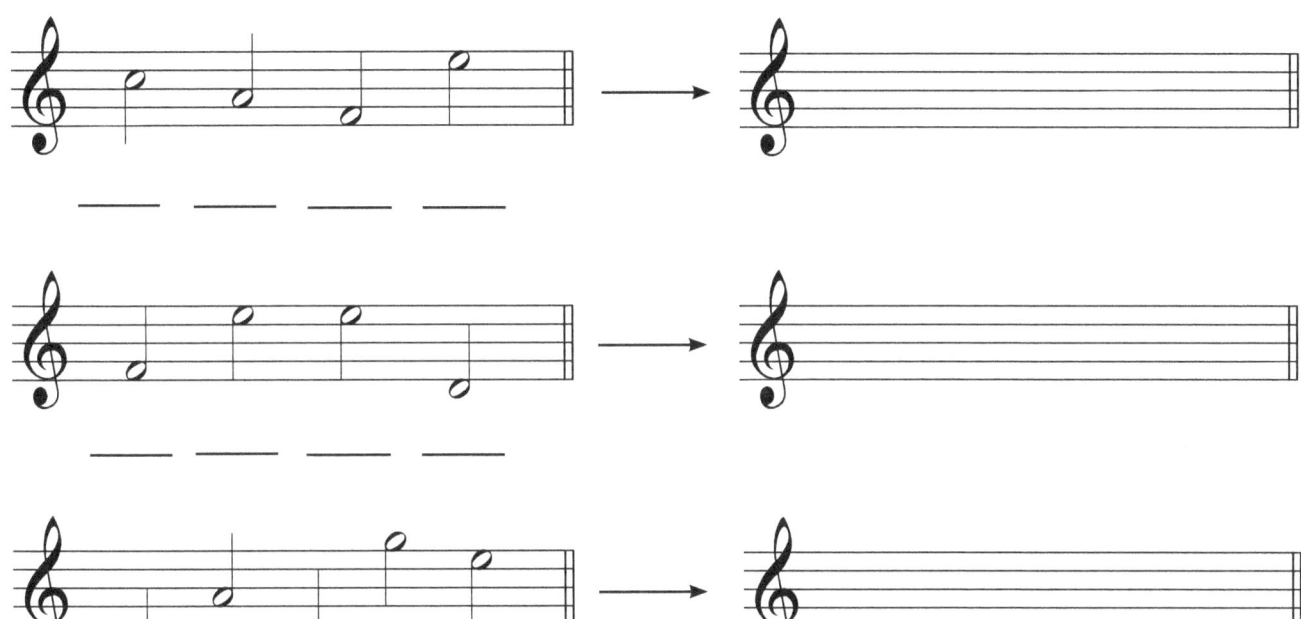

Name the following line notes which spell words. Write them again in the blank measures using only notes that are in **spaces**.

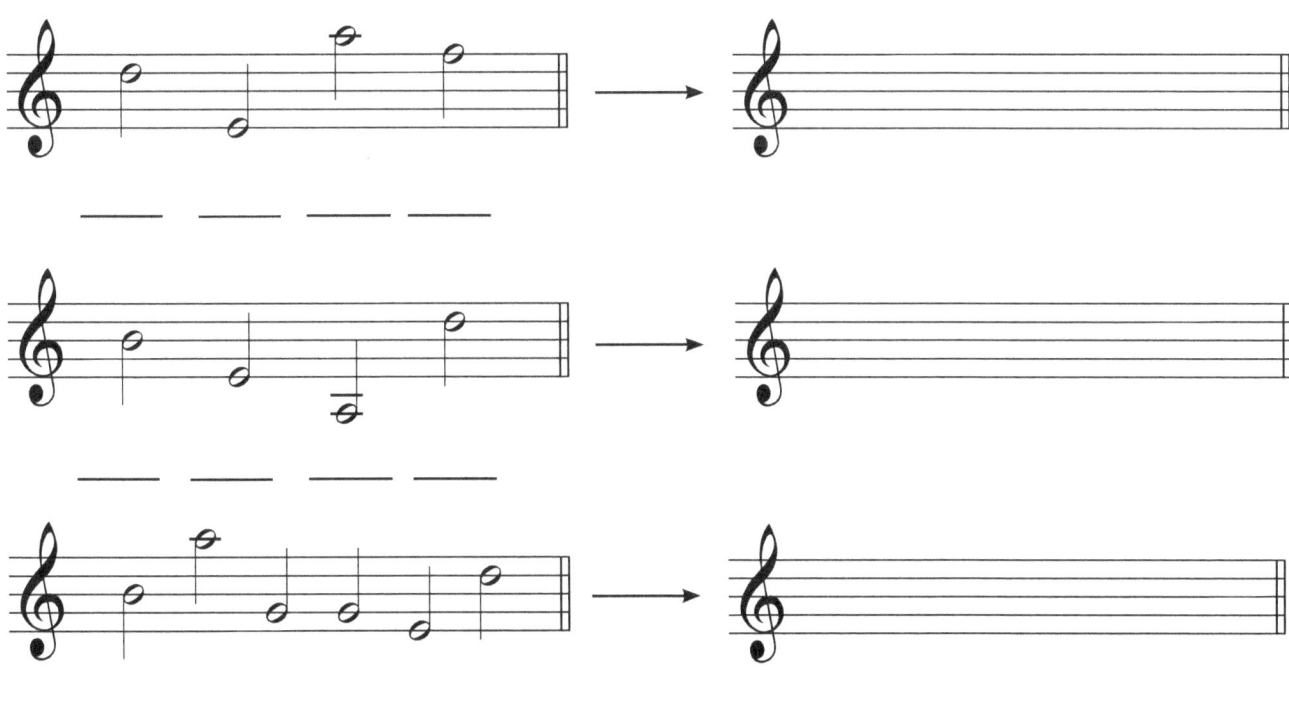

2
Note Values

The Note

Let's talk about notes in general and different types of notes. It is essential to know the various parts of a note and how they work.

The most important part of any note is the ***note head.*** The note head is the round part of the note. The note head is placed on the staff and gives us the pitch of the note. Note heads are all shaped the same. See Figure 2.1.

Figure 2.1

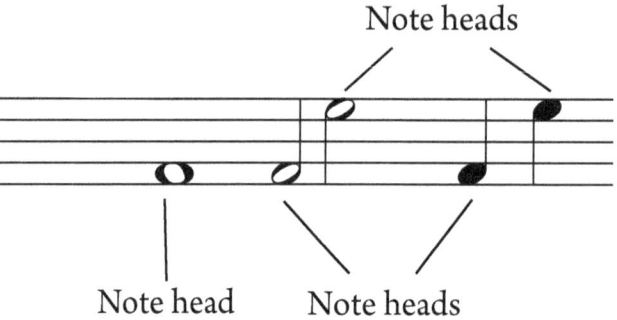

Some notes have stems. The stem is the line that goes up or down from the note head. When a stem goes up, it is placed on the right side of the note head, and when it goes down it is placed on the left side. See Figure 2.2. The length of the note stem is one octave or 8 notes.

Figure 2.2

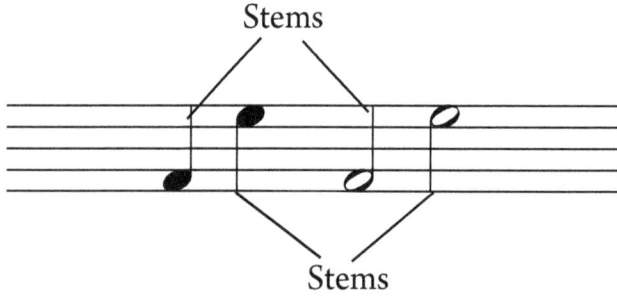

Note Values

In written music, where the note is placed on the staff indicates its pitch, but how the note looks indicates its duration, or how long you hold it. Every note has a value. It might be one beat, or four beats, or two beats. In this level, we are going to learn five different *note values*.

The Whole Note

The note head of the *whole note* is hollow, and it has no stem. This note is easy to detect because it is the only one without a stem. The whole note receives four counts, and its duration is four beats.

Figure 2.3

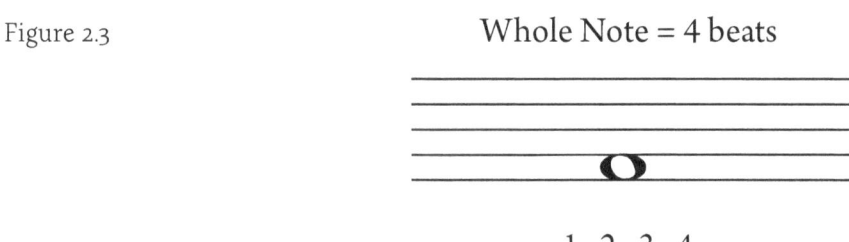

The Half Note

The *half note* is a hollow note with a stem attached. It receives two counts, and its duration is two beats.

Figure 2.4

Half Note = 2 beats

1 2

The Dotted Half Note

The **dotted half note** is a half note with a dot beside it. It receives three counts, and its duration is three beats. If the dotted note is in a space, the dot is placed in the same space as the note. If the dotted note is on a line, the dot is placed in the space above the note.

Figure 2.5

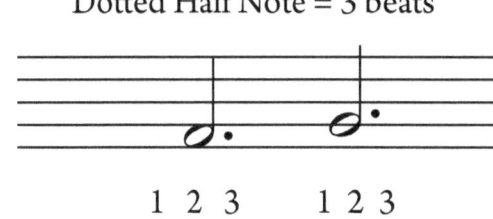

The Quarter Note

The **quarter note** has a solid note head and a stem attached. It receives one count, and its duration is one beat.

Figure 2.6

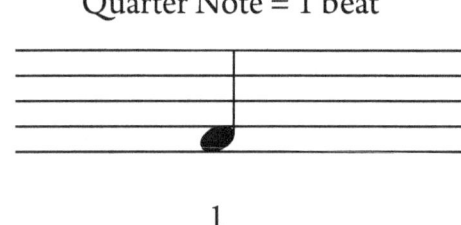

The Eighth Note

The **eighth note** looks similar to a quarter note, but its stem has an attached flag. When two or more eighth notes appear together, the flags are joined by a beam which connects the notes. If we divide the quarter note into two parts, we get eighth notes. Its duration is one half of a beat. Counting eighth notes is a little tougher than the other notes. If you have groupings of two eighth notes, you can count them "one and" with "one" for the first eighth note and "and" for the second eighth note.

Figure 2.7

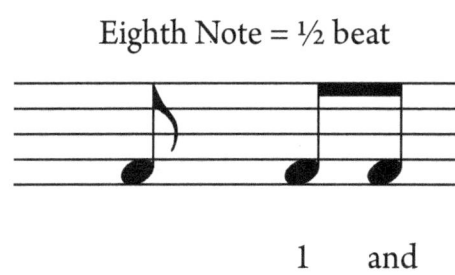

Chart of Note Values - It's relative!

Figure 2.8 shows that each note in the chart is twice the value of the one below it.

figure 2.8

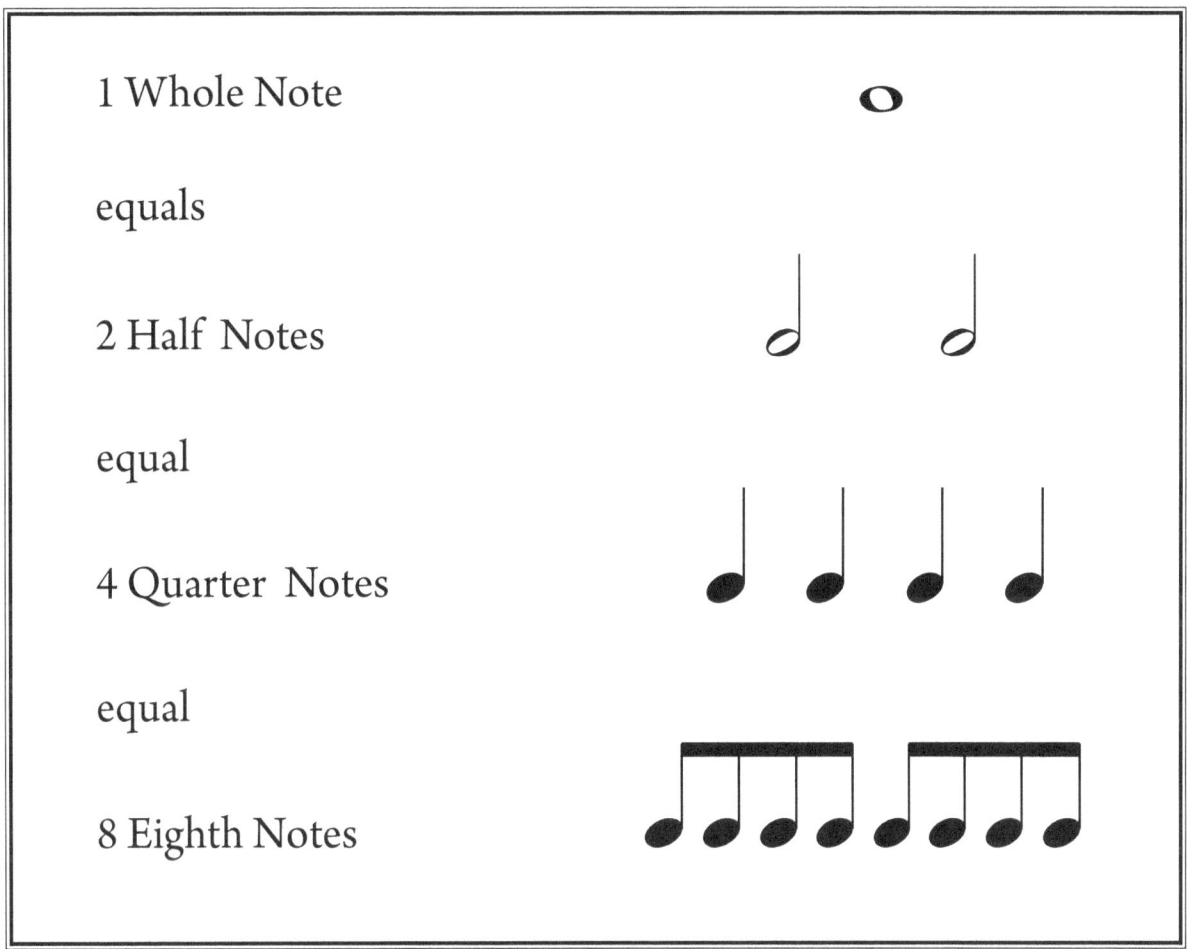

❶ 1. Name the type of note or notes.
❷
❸

2. Write the number of beats the following notes receive.

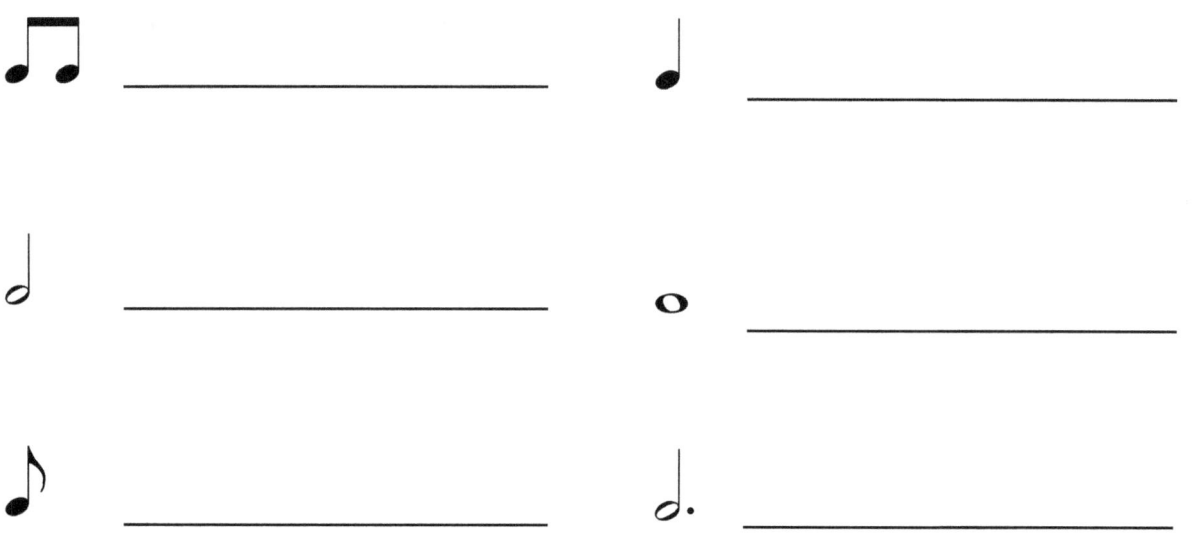

Note Values

3. Write **one** note which is equal to the following groups of notes.

Stems up? Stems down?

A note stem can go up, or a note stem can do down. For a note on the middle line, the stem may go in either direction. It usually depends on the other notes. If their stems are all going down the note on the middle line would go down. If they are going up, the note on the middle line would go up. Majority rules! However, if there is no clear majority, the stem of the note on the middle line can go in any direction you choose.

Figure 2.9 shows notes on the third line with their stems going up and down. *The length of a stem is eight notes, also called an octave.*

Figure 2.9

© San Marco Publications 2022   Note Values

If a note is below the third line, its stem goes up. Be sure to place the stem on the right side of the note when it goes up.

Figure 2.10 shows notes below the third line. The note on the third line has its stem going up. It follows the majority of the other notes whose stems also go up.

Figure 2.10

If a note is above the third line, its stem goes down. Be sure to place the stem on the left side of the note when it goes down.

Figure 2.11 shows notes above the third line. The note on the third line has its stem going down. It follows the direction of the other notes whose stems go down.

Figure 2.11

1. Add stems to the following notes.

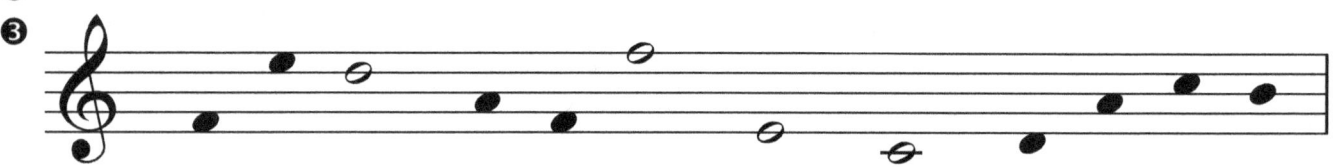

❶ When we beam a group of eighth notes sometimes one or more of the stems are placed differently
❷ than would be the case if flags were used. If most of the notes are above the third (middle) line of
❸ the staff, stems go downward (Figure 2.12 a). If most of the notes are below the third line, the stems go upward (Figure 2.12 b). Here, majority rules.

Figure 2.12

If the number of notes above the middle line of the staff is equal to the number below, the stem direction is determined by the note which is the farthest from the middle line (Figure 2.13).

Figure 2.13

❶
❷ 1. Connect each group of four eighth notes with stems and beams.
❸

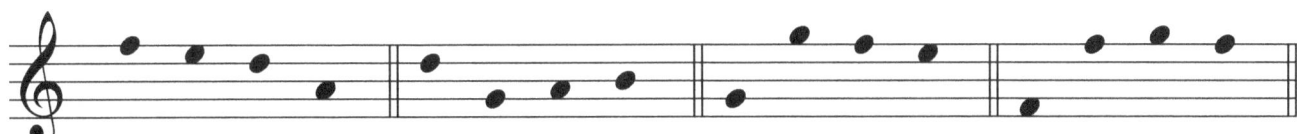

3
Rests

❶❷❸ Silence is Golden

Mozart said: "Notes are silver, rests are golden." Silence in music is as important as sound. Silence in music is shown with *rests*. The name and length of the rests are the same as the name and length of the notes we studied in the last lesson.

The Whole Rest

A whole rest is four beats long and indicates four counts of silence. The whole rest hangs from the fourth line. It is also used to indicate one whole measure of rest.

Figure 3.1

Whole Rest = 4 beats

1 2 3 4

❶❷❸ 1. Draw a line of whole rests on the staff below.

The Half Rest

A half rest is two beats long and indicates two counts of silence. The half rest sits on the third line.

Figure 3.2

1 2

2. Draw a line of half rests on the staff below.

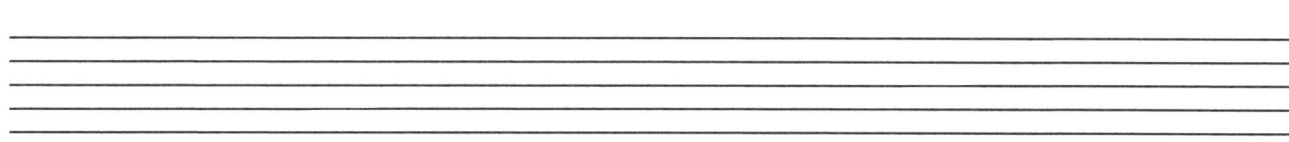

The Quarter Rest

A quarter rest is one beat long and indicates one count of silence. The quarter rest is tricky to draw. Study its shape.

Figure 3.3

1

3. Draw a line of quarter rests on the staff below.

The Eighth Rest

An eighth rest is one half of a beat in duration and indicates one half of a count of silence. The eighth rest is placed in the middle of the staff and looks a little like the number 7.

Figure 3.4

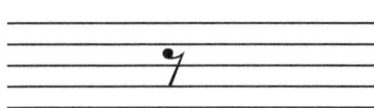

4. Draw a line of eighth rests on the staff below.

5. Name the following notes and rests.

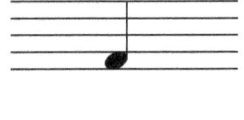

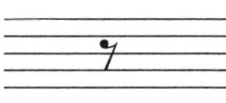

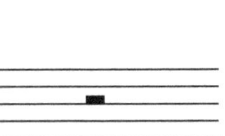

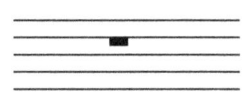

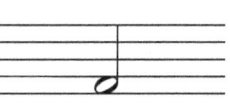

© San Marco Publications 2023

Rests

6. Draw the equivalent rest for each note.

7. Draw **one** rest which is equal to the following notes.

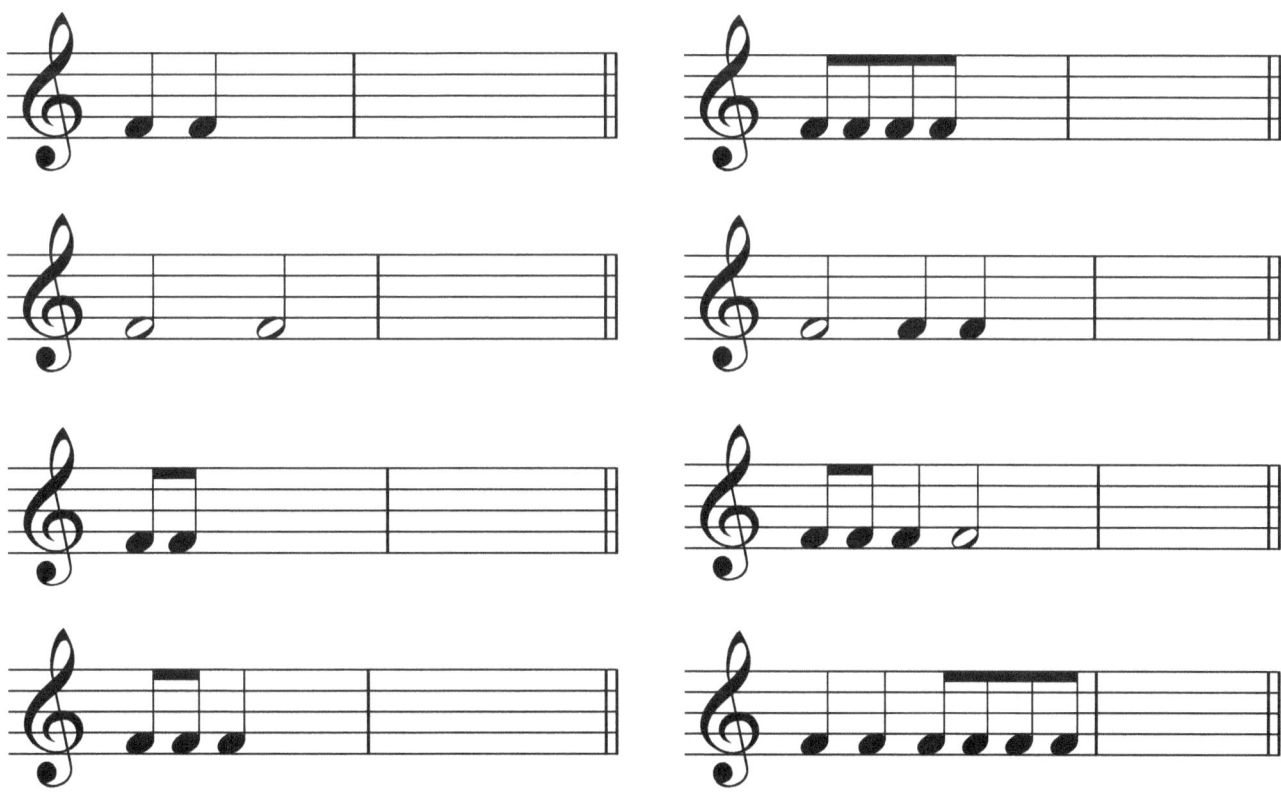

Music Terms

Music terms are used to tell a performer what to do when playing a piece of music. How loud or soft to play. How fast to play. How long or short to play a note. Most music terms are written in Italian. In the beginning of the 16th century, there was a lot of music being composed in Italy, and composers started to write directions for performing their music. These composers were Italian, so they wrote the instructions in Italian. We also see some music terms in German and French, but the majority are in Italian. It has become a universal language for music terminology.

Dynamics

Dynamics is the word used for how loud or soft we play. The two most important words dealing with dynamics are *piano* (soft) and *forte* (loud). Almost all other dynamics are related to these two words. Study Figure 3.5 which is a chart of dynamic markings.

Figure 3.5

ITALIAN TERM	ABBREVIATION	MEANING
piano	*p*	soft
mezzo piano	*mp*	medium soft
mezzo forte	*mf*	medium loud
forte	*f*	loud

In the 19th century, composers started writing music that had sections that gradually grew louder or became softer. The Italian term for growing louder is **crescendo**. The Italian word for becoming softer is **decrescendo** or **diminuendo**. These terms may be abbreviated as **cresc., decresc.** or **dim.** Figure 3.6 shows the diagrams that represent **crescendo** and **decrescendo**.

Figure 3.6

crescendo   *decrescendo*

4
Meter

Bar Lines

The staff is divided into sections by vertical lines called **bar lines**. There are single bar lines and double bar lines. A double bar line indicates the end of a section or the end of a piece of music. You cannot hear a bar line. Its purpose is to make the music easier to read by dividing the music into smaller units or sections.

Figure 4.1

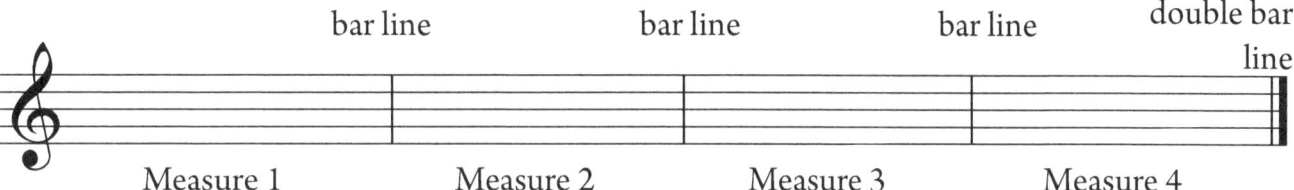

Measures

Bar lines divide the music into sections called **measures**. Figure 4.1 contains four measures. Measures may be different sizes depending upon the amount of beats and notes in the measure.

Time Signatures

Two numbers are placed at the beginning of every piece of music. These numbers are called the **time signature** or **meter**. The time signature tells you how many beats are in each measure. It also shows you which kind of note gets one beat.

Figure 4.2

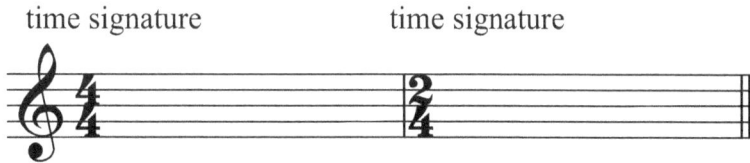

The Top Number

The top number of the time signature indicates how many beats will be in each measure. In the example in Figure 4.3, 4/4 time has four beats in each measure.

Figure 4.3

The Bottom Number

The bottom number of the time signature indicates which note receives one beat. The 4 at the bottom of the time signature in Figure 4.3 means that the quarter note receives one beat. In 4/4 time every measure adds up to four quarter notes. In 2/4 time each measure adds up to two quarter notes. There can be different numbers at the bottom number of a time signature, but 4 is the most common. In this level, we will be studying time signatures which have 4 on the bottom.

4/4 Time

There are many different time signatures. The most common is 4/4. The reason we have different time signatures or meters is that different types of music fall into different patterns. Sometimes words of a song help to shape the patterns in music. A four beat pattern indicates 4/4 time or a two beat pattern indicates 2/4 time. Figure 4.4 is an example where the words to the song help to dictate the time signature. This song has a definite four beats per measure pattern.

Figure 4.4

❶ ❷ ❸ Common Time

4/4 time is so common you will often see it abbreviated with the letter "C" instead of the numbers 4/4. The C stands for *common* and is shown in Figure 4.5.

Figure 4.5

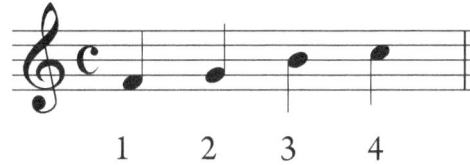

2/4 Time

For the time signature 2/4, there are two beats in each measure and the quarter note receives one beat. Figure 4.6 is an example of 2/4 time where the words to the song help to dictate the time signature. This song has a clear two beats per measure pattern.

Figure 4.6

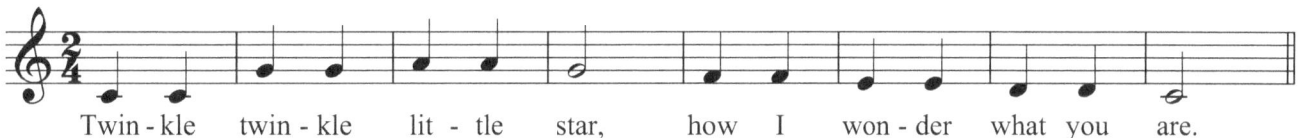

❶ ❷ ❸ 1. Write the beats according to the time signatures under each measure.

3/4 Time

In 3/4 time, there are three beats in each measure and the quarter note receives one beat. Figure 4.7 is an example of 3/4 time where the words to the song help to dictate the time signature. 3/4 time is sometimes known as waltz time because a waltz requires three beats per measure in order to dance to it.

Figure 4.7

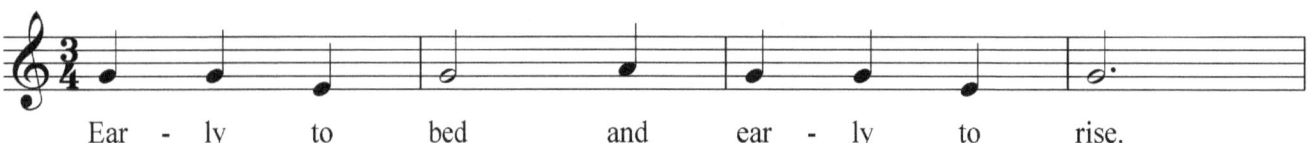

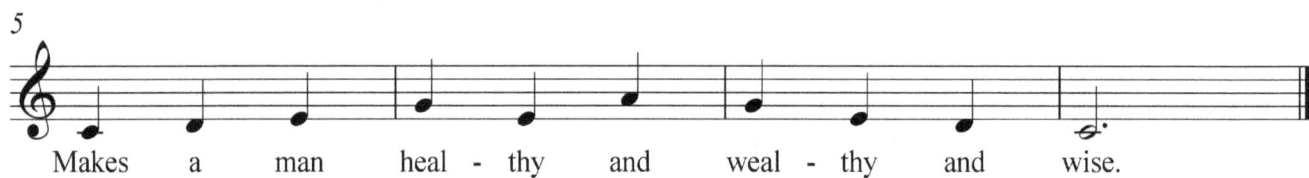

1. Add **one** note to complete each measure according to the given time signatures.

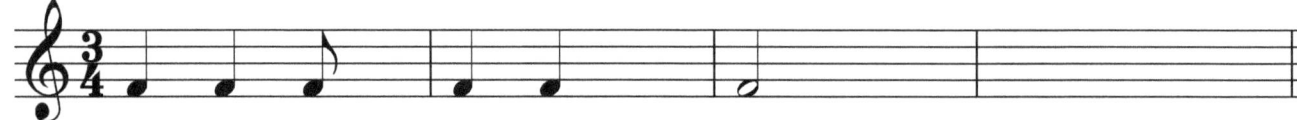

❶ 2. Add time signatures to the following lines.
❷
❸

3. Add bar lines according to the given time signatures.

❶ 4. Add **one note** to complete each measure according to the given time signatures.
❷
❸

5. Add **one rest** to complete each measure according to the given time signatures.

Tied Notes

A ***tie*** is a curved line which connects two notes of the same pitch. The time values of tied notes are added together to make a longer note - you only play the note once.

*Be careful not to confuse ties and slurs! A tie looks like a **slur** - but a slur connects two notes of a different pitch and indicates that the notes are to be played smoothly.* Figure 4.8 shows two tied Fs; the second example shows an F slurred to a G.

Figure 4.8

One reason we use a tie is to hold a note across a bar line. In Figure 4.9 the G is held for three beats.

Figure 4.9

Ties are usually written on the opposite side of a musical note to its stem. In Figure 4.10, the Fs are written stems up, so the tie is drawn below the notes. The Es have stems down, so the ties are drawn above the notes.

Figure 4.10

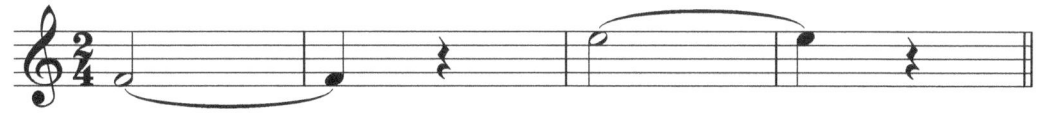

❶ 1. Write the counts under each measure. State how many beats each tied note receives. The first
❷   one is started for you.
❸

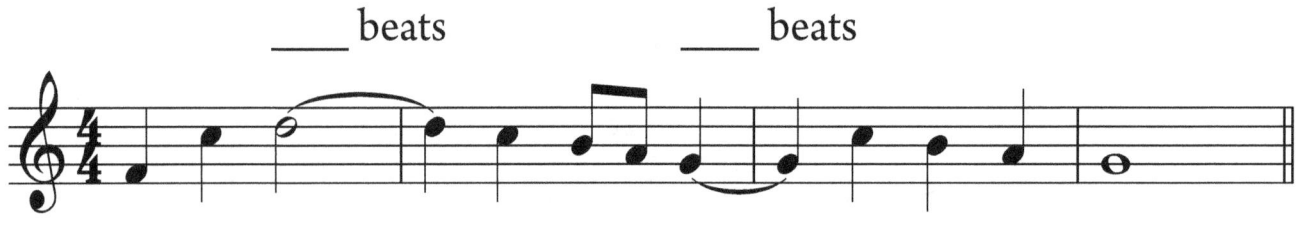

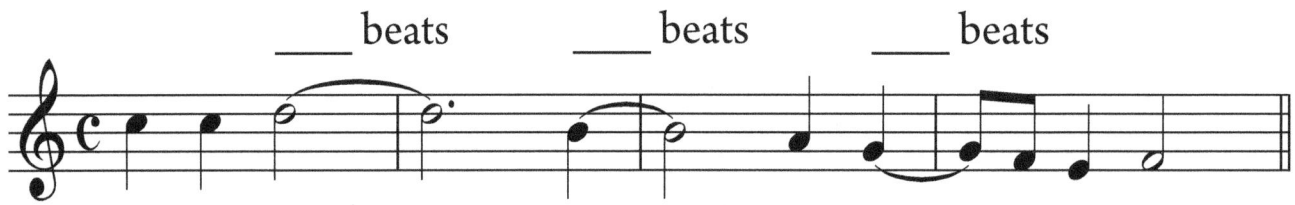

Dotted Notes

A dot to the right of a note makes it last longer. A dot adds half the value to a note. In this level, we will study dotted half and quarter notes.

❶❷❸ The Dotted Half Note

A half note gets 2 beats. The dot is worth half of that. Half of 2 is 1 (2 + 1 = 3). This gives us a total of three. A ***dotted half note*** gets three beats. Figure 2.2 contains a dotted half note.

Figure 4.11

When drawing a dot beside a note in a space, the dot should be placed in the same space as the note. For a line note, the dot is placed in the space above the line note.
Figure 4.12 shows a dotted space and dotted line note.

Figure 4.12

❷❸ The Dotted Quarter Note

A quarter note gets one beat. The dot is worth half of that. Half of 1 is ½ (1 + ½ = 1½). This is a total of one and a half. A ***dotted quarter note*** gets one and a half beats. When counting the dotted quarter it is easier to think of it as equal to three eighth notes. It helps to divide each beat using the word *and* to represent the eighth notes.

Figure 4.13

❷ 1. Add bar lines to complete the following according to the time signatures.
❸

❷ 2. In the empty measure write **one** note that is equal to the following groups of notes.
❸

❷❸ Rest Review

Silence in music is as important as sound. A ***rest*** is used to show silence in music. Figure 4.14 shows the rests covered so far. The whole rest is equal to one complete measure of rest. In 4/4 time it's value is 4 beats, in 3/4 time it is worth 3 beats, in 2/4 time it is worth 2 beats. This rest is used to represent one complete measure of silence no matter what the time signature.

Figure 4.14

Whole Rest	𝄻	4 beats or one bar of rest
Half Rest	𝄼	2 beats
Quarter Rest	𝄽	1 beat
Eighth Rest	𝄾	½ beat

❷ 1. Add **one** rest to complete each measure according to the time signature.
❸

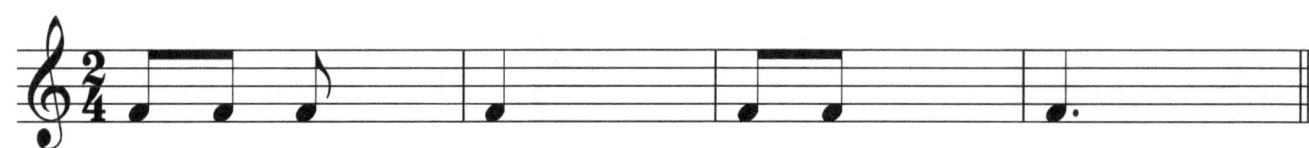

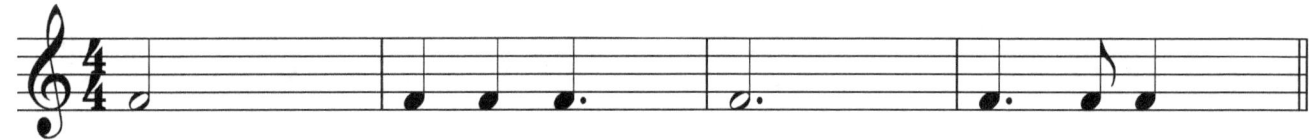

2. Add **one** note to complete each measure according to the time signature.

❸ The Sixteenth Note

There are 16 sixteenth notes in a whole note. This makes the sixteenth note ¼ of a beat. One quarter note is equal to 4 sixteenth notes. A single sixteenth note has two flags attached to the stem. These flags are always placed on the right of the stem. When sixteenth notes are grouped together their stems are joined by two beams. Figure 4.15 show single sixteenth notes with flags and groups of sixteenth notes joined by beams.

Figure 4.15

Counting Sixteenth Notes

When we write sixteenth notes the beat is split up into four parts. We can assign each part a word or name. When you count say: 1 ee and ah (1 e + a). This divides the beat into four equal sections. Figure 4.16 shows a measure of sixteenth notes with counting.

Figure 4.16

The Sixteenth Rest

A sixteenth rest looks like eighth rest with an extra flag on it. The flags are placed in the second and third space of the staff. This rest has the same value as a sixteenth note, ¼ of a beat

Figure 4.17

❸ 1. Circle the note or rest with the shortest duration.

2. Circle the note or rest with the longest duration.

❸ Joining Notes

Notes with flags are usually grouped together with beams to show one beat. Figure 4.18 shows how notes are grouped with beams to indicate one complete beat.

Figure 4.18

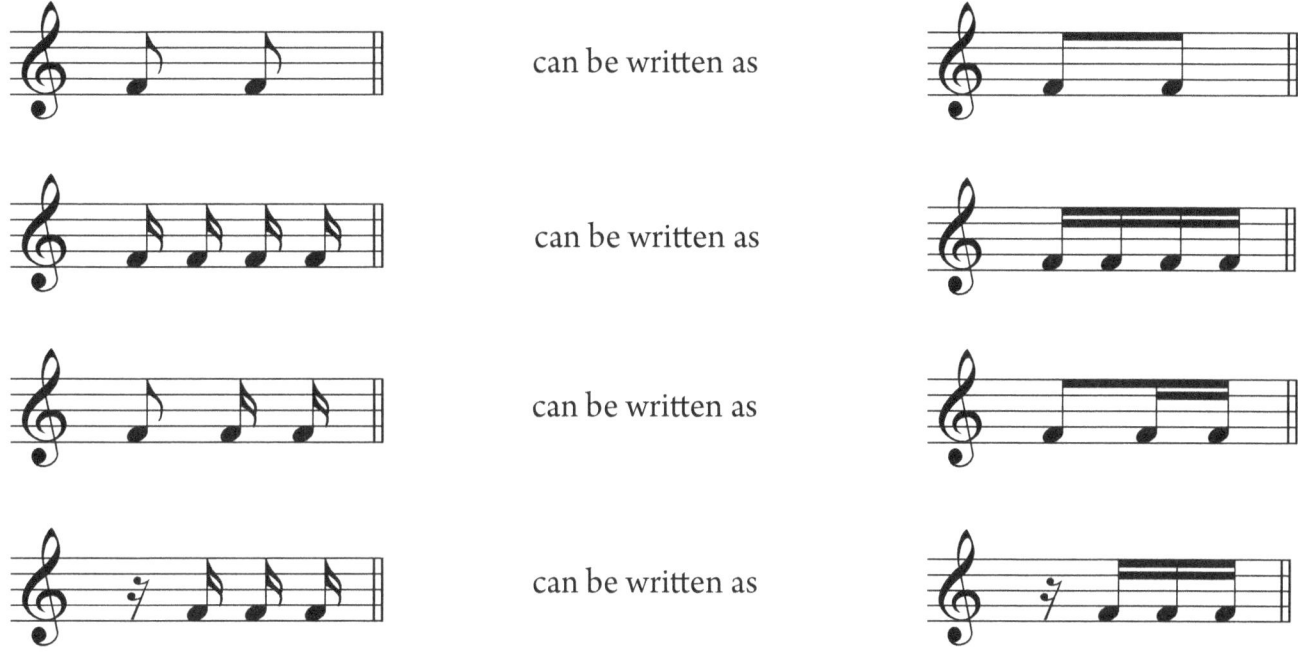

❸ 1. Rewrite the following joining the notes with beams wherever possible.

❸ 2. Answer the following questions.

a) A whole note equals how many half notes? _____

b) A half note equals how many quarter notes? _____

c) A quarter note equals how many eighth notes? _____

d) A quarter note equals how many sixteenth notes? _____

e) An eighth note equals how many sixteenth notes? _____

3. Write **one** note which is equal to the following groups of notes.

❸ 4. Add time signatures at the beginning of each line.

5. Add **one** rest to complete each measure.

❸ Dotted Eighth Notes

A dot after a note increases its value by half. Figure 4.19 contains a dotted half worth 3 beats and a dotted quarter worth 1 ½ beats.

Figure 4.19

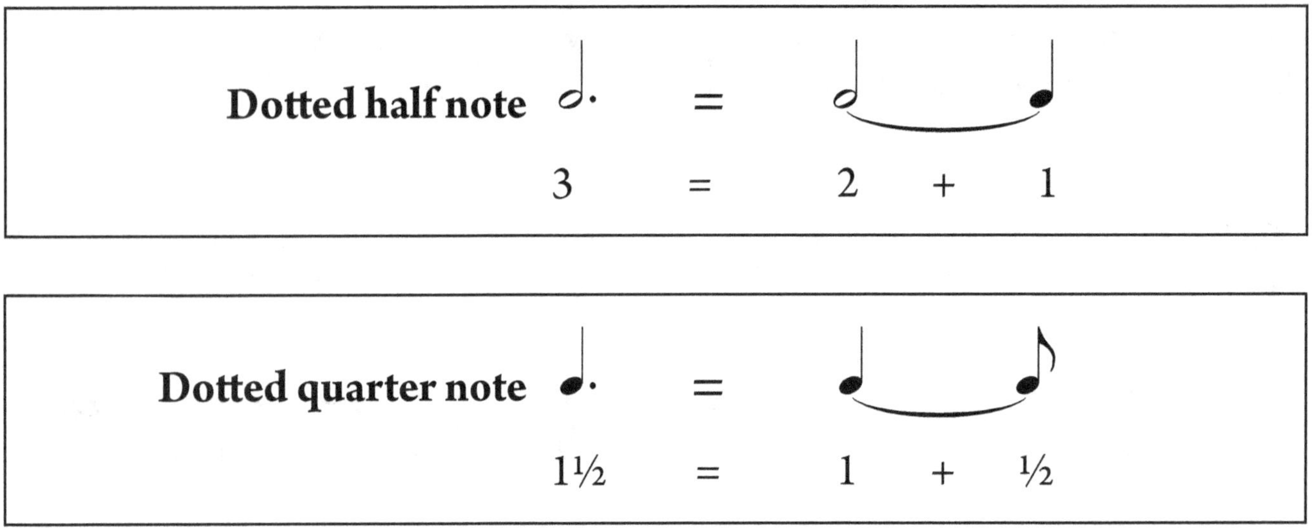

Dotted half note 𝅗𝅥. = 𝅗𝅥 ⌣ 𝅘𝅥

3 = 2 + 1

Dotted quarter note 𝅘𝅥. = 𝅘𝅥 ⌣ 𝅘𝅥𝅮

1½ = 1 + ½

Figure 4.20 contains a dotted eighth note. An eighth note is worth ½ of a beat. The dot is equal to a sixteenth note. A sixteenth note is worth ¼ of a beat. The dotted eighth is equal to ¾ of a beat.

Figure 4.20

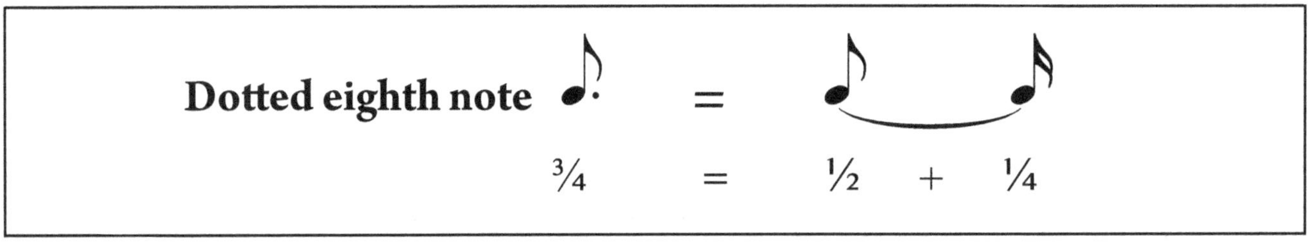

Dotted eighth note 𝅘𝅥𝅮. = 𝅘𝅥𝅮 ⌣ 𝅘𝅥𝅯

¾ = ½ + ¼

Think of a dotted eighth note like a pie. The whole pie is 1 beat. An eighth note is ½ of the pie and a sixteenth note is ¼ of the pie. A dotted eighth (½ + ¼) is ¾ of the pie, or ¾ of a beat.

Figure 4.21

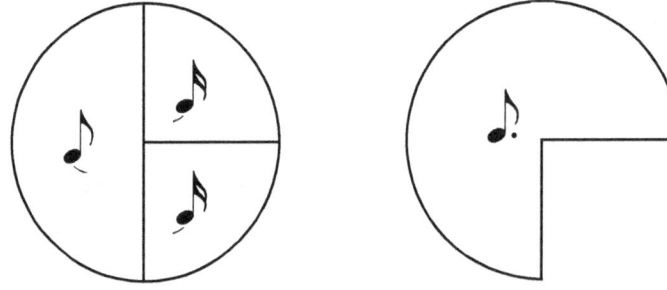

❸ The dotted eighth note is often seen in combination with a sixteenth note as shown in Figure 4.22. The dotted eighth is connected by a beam to a sixteenth note. This creates one complete beat and is a common rhythmic figure.

Figure 4.22

1. Draw a line connecting each group of notes with its corresponding note value.

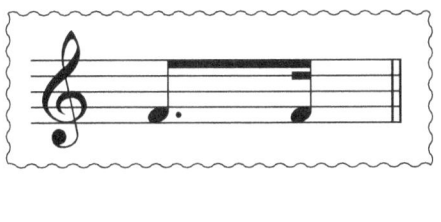   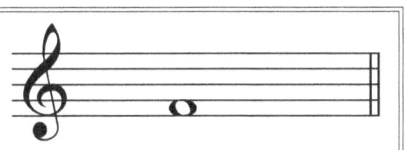

   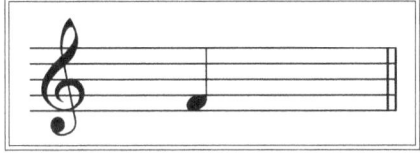

   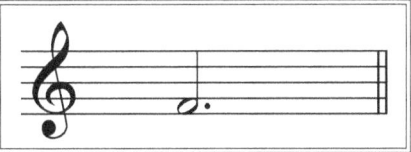

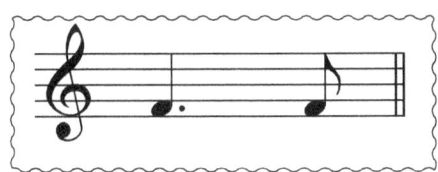   

Meter

❸ 2. Add the missing bar lines to the following musical examples.

❸ The Upbeat or Anacrusis

The first beat of a measure is the strongest and is called the **downbeat**. Some pieces begin on an unaccented or less strong beat. This is called an ***upbeat, pickup,*** or ***anacrusis***.

When a melody begins on an upbeat, both the first and last measure will be incomplete. Figure 4.23 contains a melody that begins on an upbeat. It begins on beat 3, a weak beat. The first note of this melody is a quarter note upbeat. The first and last measures of this melody are incomplete. The third beat which is missing from the last measure is equal to the upbeat in the first measure. These two incomplete measures add up to one complete measure. No rests are needed with incomplete measures.

4..23

American Folk Song

❸ Review - The Phrase

Most traditional melodies move in four measure sections called ***phrases***. A phrase is a musical sentence. Like the sentence in a story, a phrase represents one musical idea. Phrases are often indicated by a long curved line called a ***phrase mark***. A phrase mark looks like a large slur. This line indicates the beginning and end of the phrase. Figure 4.23 has phrase marks above the melody. This melody consists of two four measures phrases.

In Figure 4.23 each 4 measure phrase begins with an upbeat. When a piece begins with an upbeat, often each of the following phrases will also begin with an upbeat. This is a feature which unifies the music.

Measure numbers are an important feature in music. They help us when learning, analyzing, or rehearsing. In a piece that begins with an incomplete measure, the incomplete measure is not numbered. The first measure (m.1), is the bar after the anacrusis. This measure contains the first strong beat in the piece and is considered m.1. See Figure 4.23.

❸ 1. Name the key of the following melodies. Find and circle the upbeats (anacrusis) in each one. Mark the phrases with a slur.

Allegretto

key:

Allegro

key:

Rests in Simple Time

The time signatures we have studied, 2/4, 3/4, and 4/4, are considered *simple time* signatures. In simple time each beat can be divided evenly into 2, or 4.

When writing rests in simple time, any incomplete beats must be completed first. Figure 4.24 illustrates how to complete single quarter note beats in simple time.

Figure 4.24 a) and b): An eighth note requires an eighth rest to complete the quarter note beat.
Figure 4.24 c): Each part of the beat is completed before beginning the next part.
Figure 4.24 d): The beat is completed in order, with the 16th note and rest occuring together.
Figure 4.24 e): A dotted eighth requires a 16th rest to complete the beat.

Figure 4.24

There are specific rules for adding rests to a measure in simple time. It is important to show each beat as clearly as possible. Each beat or each part of the beat must be completed before beginning the next beat. In Figure 4.25 measure 2, each eighth note beat is completed with an eighth note rest. In measures 3 and 4, the sixteenth note has a sixteenth rest to complete part of the beat and then an eighth rest to complete the remainder of the beat.

Figure 4.25

❸ In 3/4 time each beat or part of the beat should be completed first. Join beats 1 and 2, a strong and weak beat, into one rest. **Do not join beats 2 and 3, two weak beats, into one rest.** Never join two weak beats into one rest.

Figure 4.26

We never use rests larger than one beat unless it is in the first half or last half of a measure in 4/4 time. Never join beats 2 and 3, a weak beat and a medium beat, into one rest. As in all simple time signatures, finish any incomplete beats first.

Figure 4.27

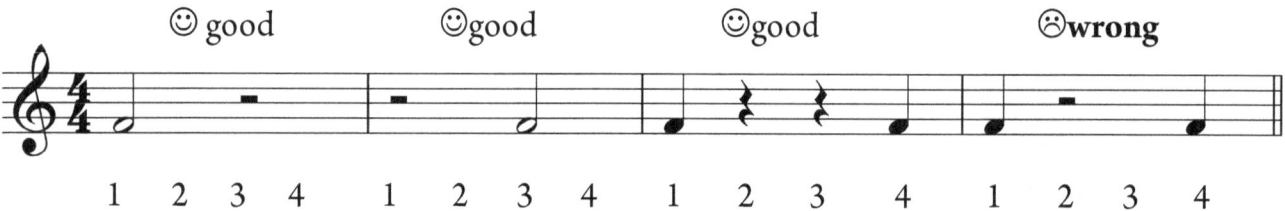

In 2/4, 3/4, and 4/4 time the whole rest is used to show one complete measure of silence. Always use a whole rest to indicate a whole measure of silence in these time signatures.

Figure 4.28

> *We have not studied dotted rests since they are not used in simple time. Dotted notes are fine, but never use dotted rests in 2/4, 3/4, or 4/4 time. Dotted rests will be covered later.*

❸1. Complete each quarter note beat by adding rests under the brackets.

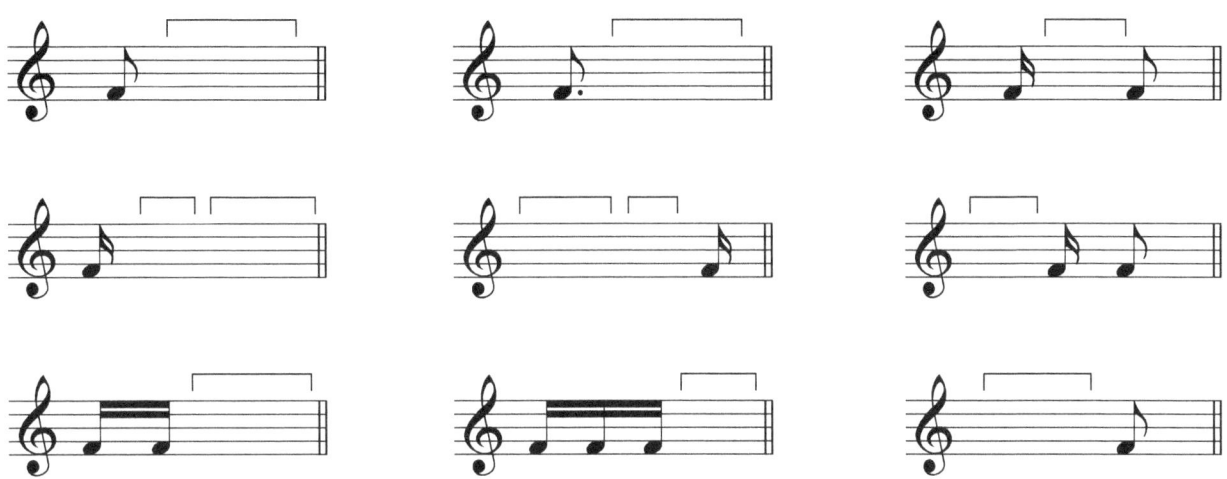

2. Mark each measure in the following examples as ☑ if the rests are correct, or ☒ if the rests are incorrect.

3. Add one rest under each bracket to complete the following measures.

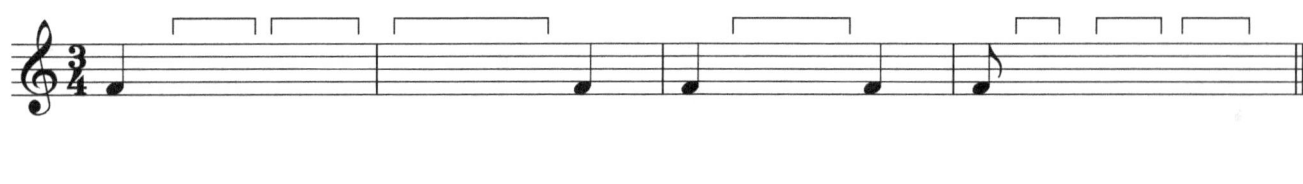

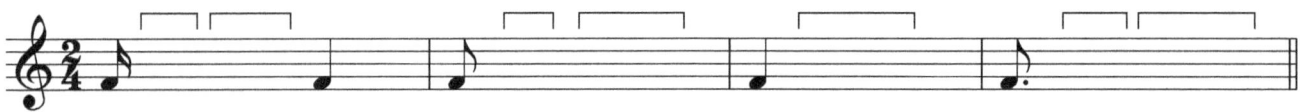

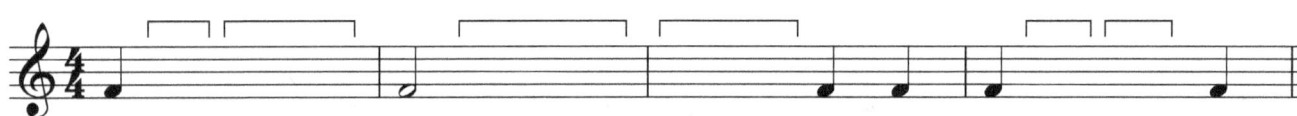

4. Add rests under the brackets to complete each measure. There may be more than one rest under each bracket.

❸ Music Signs

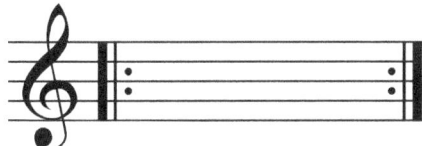

repeat marks - at the second sign go back to the first sign and repeat the music from there. The first sign is left out if the music is repeated from the beginning.

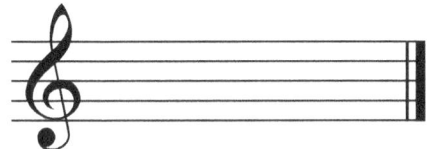

double barline - indicates the end of a piece of music.

tenuto mark - when placed over or under a note, hold it for its full value.

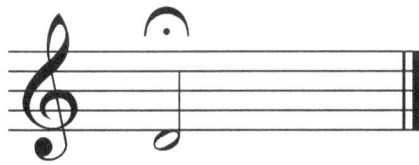

fermata - pause, hold note or rest longer than its written value.

pedal symbol - press/release the right pedal.

5
Accidentals

❶❷❸ Whole Steps and Half Steps

In the music we are studying, the smallest distance between two notes is a ***half step***. On the keyboard, it is the distance from one key to the next closest key, black or white. This may mean a white key to a black key, a black key to a white key, or sometimes a white key to a white key. There is a half step between the two white keys E and F and B and C. With these notes there is no black key involved.

A ***whole step*** is twice as big as a half step. A whole step consists of two keys with another key, black or white, between them.

Figure 5.1 shows a few half and whole steps on the keyboard. The reason we use the keyboard as a reference is because all the notes are arranged in a simple, easy to understand way. For example, a half step is two adjacent keys on the keyboard. We will learn that almost all white keys are natural notes and black keys are notes with accidentals.

Figure 5.1

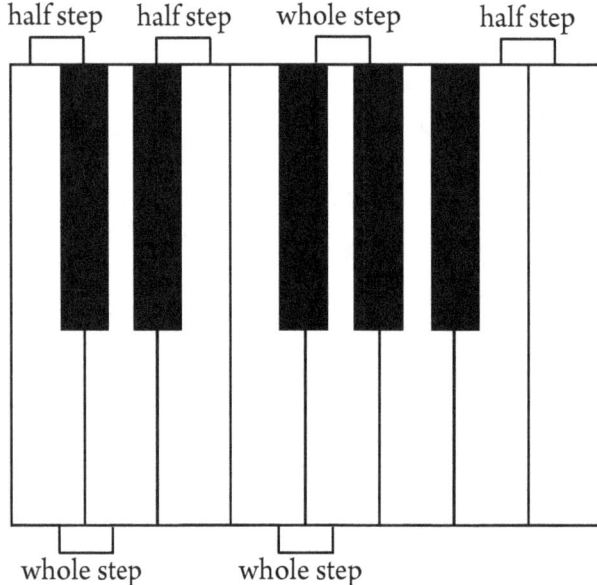

Pitch

The pitch (how high or low it sounds) of a note can be changed. We use symbols placed in front of the note called *accidentals* to raise or lower its pitch.

There are three types of accidentals: ***sharps, flats,*** and ***naturals***. These are shown in Figure 5.2.

Figure 5.2

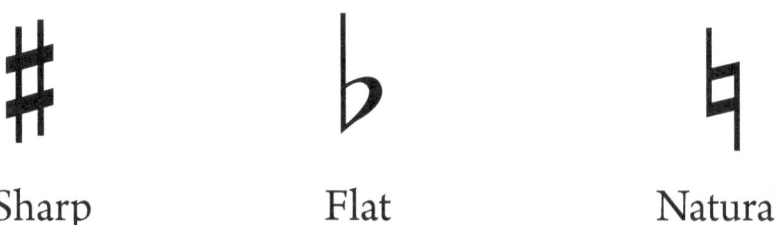

Accidentals are placed in front of the note that they alter. It is essential to place the accidental before the note, not after it. This can be confusing because when you talk about an accidental you say *"F sharp"*, but when you write it on the music score you write it sharp F. See Figure 5.3.

Figure 5.3

F sharp

When you write an accidental it should be written in the same space or on the same line as the note it is altering. Sharps, flats, and naturals have an open space that is placed in the same space or on the same line as the note they are altering.

The Sharp

A ***sharp*** is an accidental that raises the pitch of a note one half step. It looks like a number symbol. The square in the middle of the sharp should be centered on the same line or space as the note. A sharp sign can go in front of any note. Figure 5.4 contains the sharps located on the black keys of the keyboard.

Figure 5.4

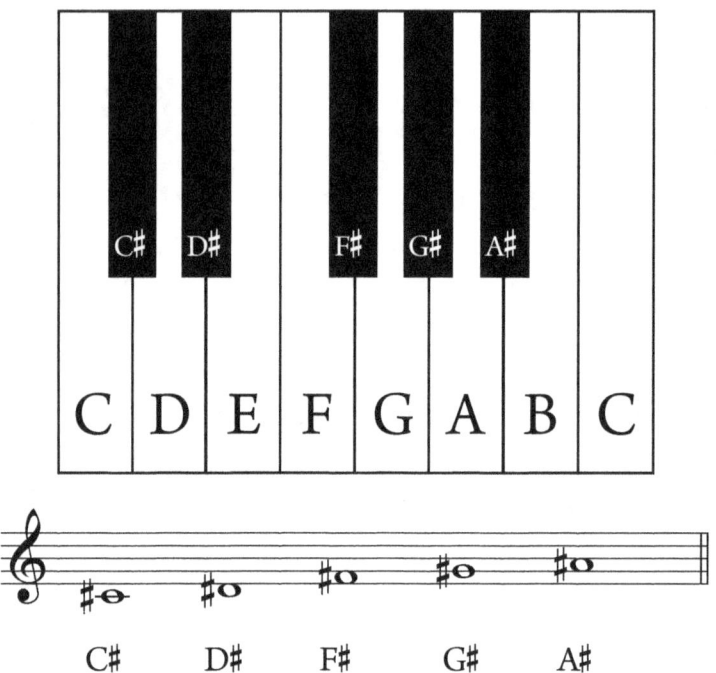

1. Write the following notes. Use whole notes.

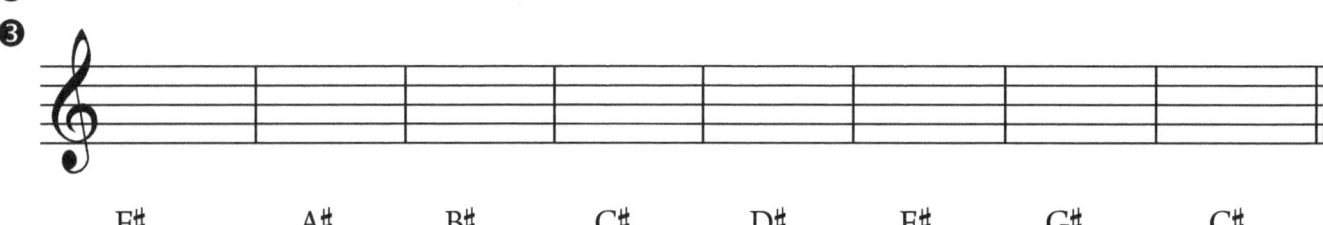

F#   A#   B#   C#   D#   E#   G#   C#

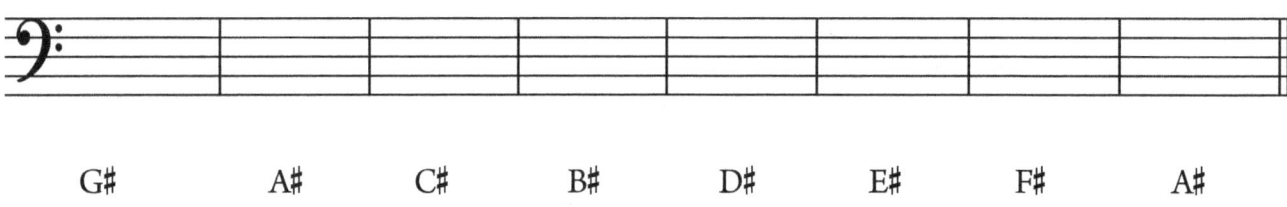

G#   A#   C#   B#   D#   E#   F#   A#

Accidentals

The Flat

A *flat* is an accidental that lowers the pitch of a note one half step. Flats look similar to the letter b. The open part of the flat sits directly on the same line or in the same space as the note that it is altering. Flat signs can be used on any note. Figure 5.5 contains the flats located on the black keys of the keyboard.

Figure 5.5

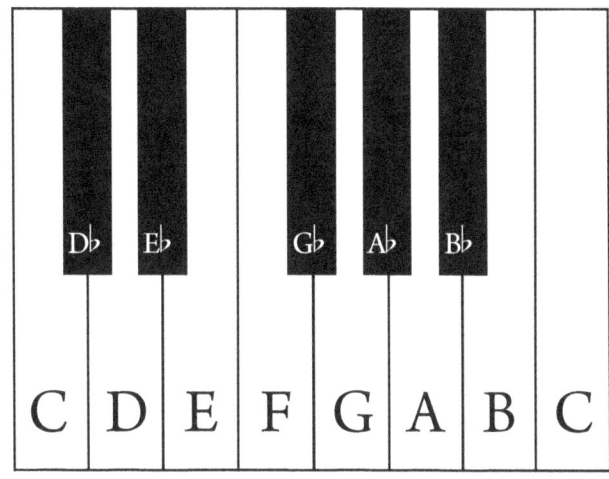

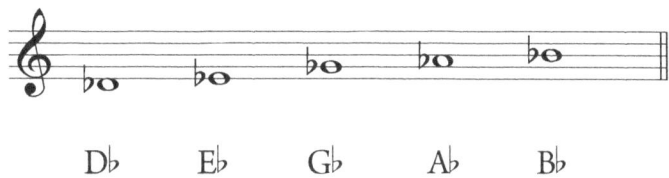

2. Write the following notes. Use whole notes.

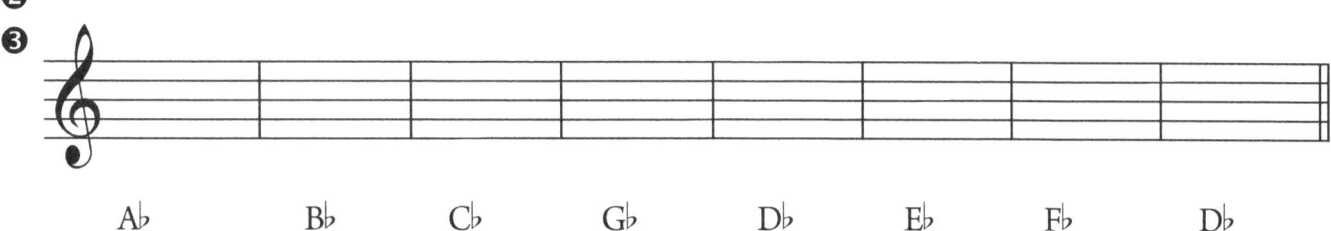

The Natural

A ***natural*** cancels a flat or sharp. If a note does not have an accidental, it is natural already. When there are not any sharps or flats, the natural is not used. The natural can raise or lower the pitch of a note. If it cancels a flat, it raises a note. If it cancels a sharp, it lowers a note. A natural sign can be used on any note. Figure 5.6 contains naturals on the treble staff.

Figure 5.6

Enharmonic Notes

You can see that each black key can have two names. One sharp name and one flat name. When you have two notes that sound the same or have the same pitch, but different names, they are called ***enharmonic notes***. This also applies to some of the white keys. Figure 5.7 contains a keyboard showing enharmonic notes. Notice the enharmonic white keys.

Figure 5.7

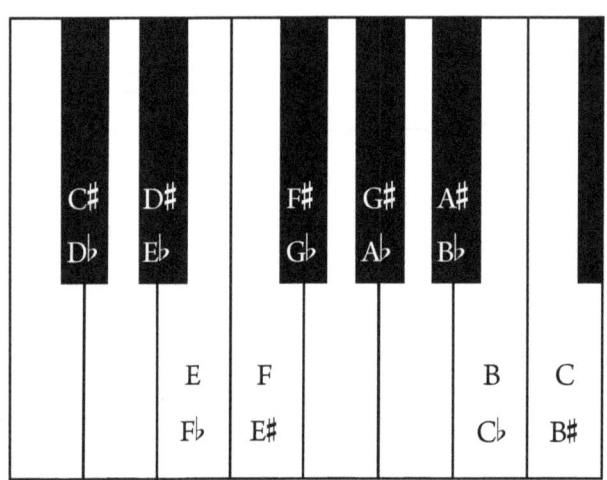

❶
❷ 3. Draw lines matching the enharmonic notes.
❸

❶
❷ How to Use Accidentals
❸

If an accidental occurs in a measure, it is good for the entire measure. However, a bar line cancels an accidental. In Figure 5.8 the B♭ lasts for the entire measure even though the flat sign is only written once. When the bar line occurs, the B is no longer flat.

Figure 5.8

When a note has the same letter name but is at a different pitch, the accidental is written again.
In Figure 5.9 the F♯ an octave higher than the first one must be written again.

Figure 5.9

accidental written again

A note with an accidental tied over the bar line is not written again.

Figure 5.10

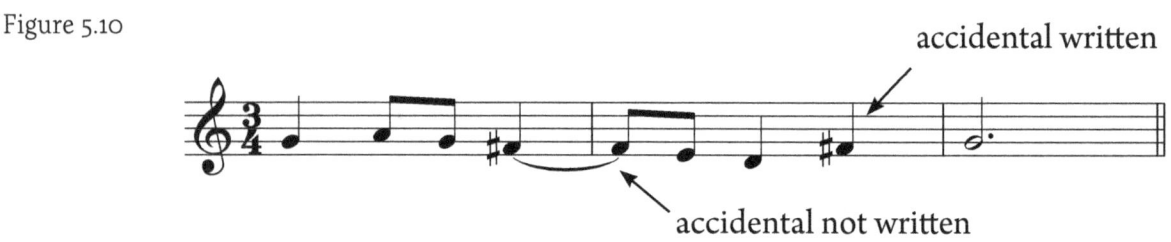

accidental written

accidental not written

Writing Half and Whole Steps

A half step can be written above or below a note using the same letter name for both notes.

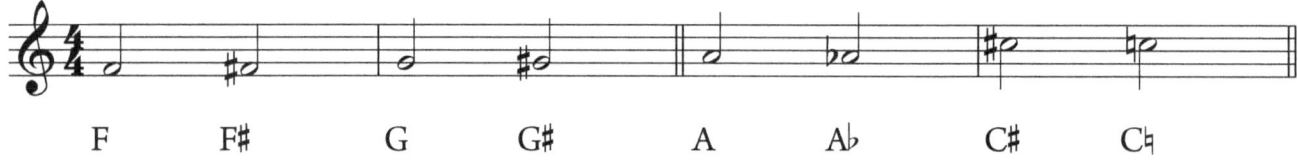

F   F♯   G   G♯   A   A♭   C♯   C♮

A half step can be written above or below a note using different letter names for the notes.

G   A♭   B   C   A   G♯   F   E

A whole step is always written using two different letter names in alphabetical order.

G   A   B   C♯   A♭   G♭   C♯   D♯

1. Name the following notes.

2. Write these notes in both clefs. Use half notes.

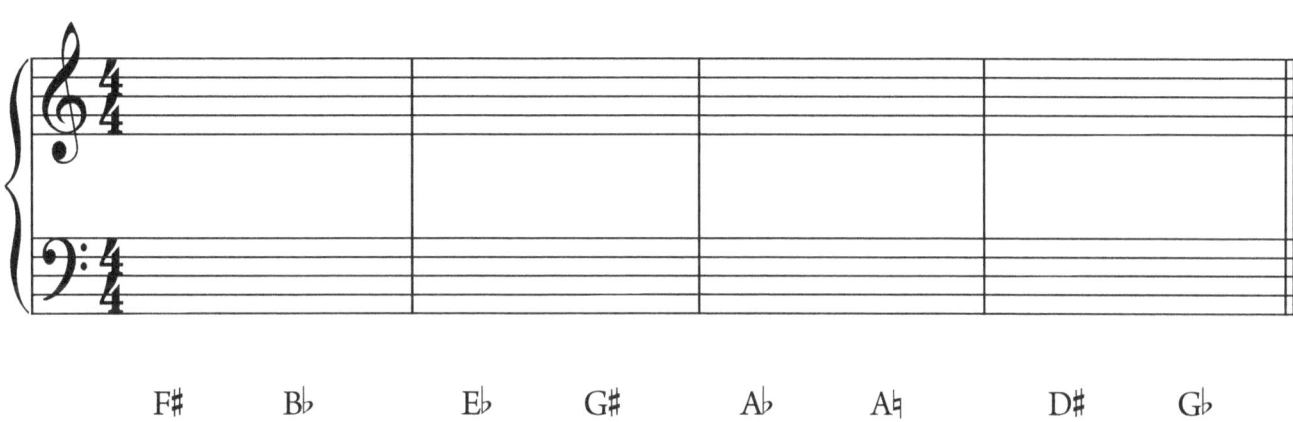

F#   B♭   E♭   G#   A♭   A♮   D#   G♭

3. Write these notes in both clefs. Use quarter notes.

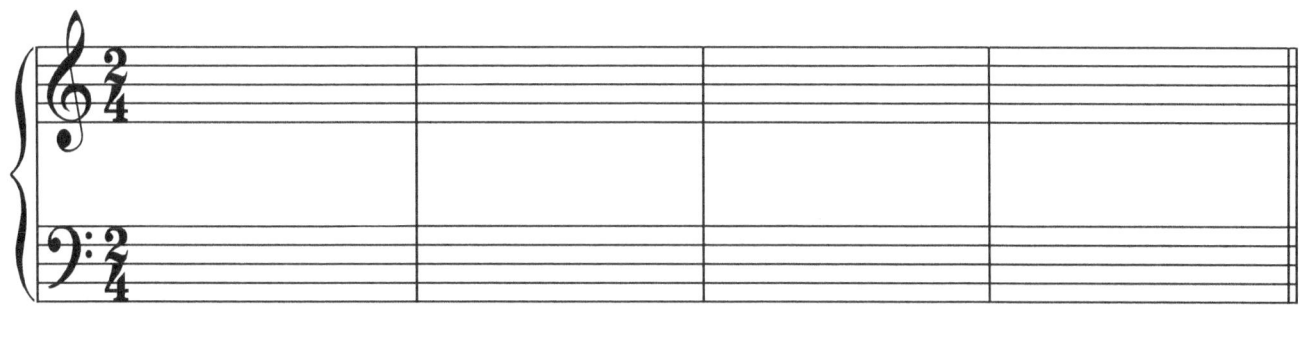

A#   D♭   F♭   F♮   C♭   B#   B♭   A♭

❶ 4. Name each note and draw a line to the correct key on the keyboard.
❷
❸

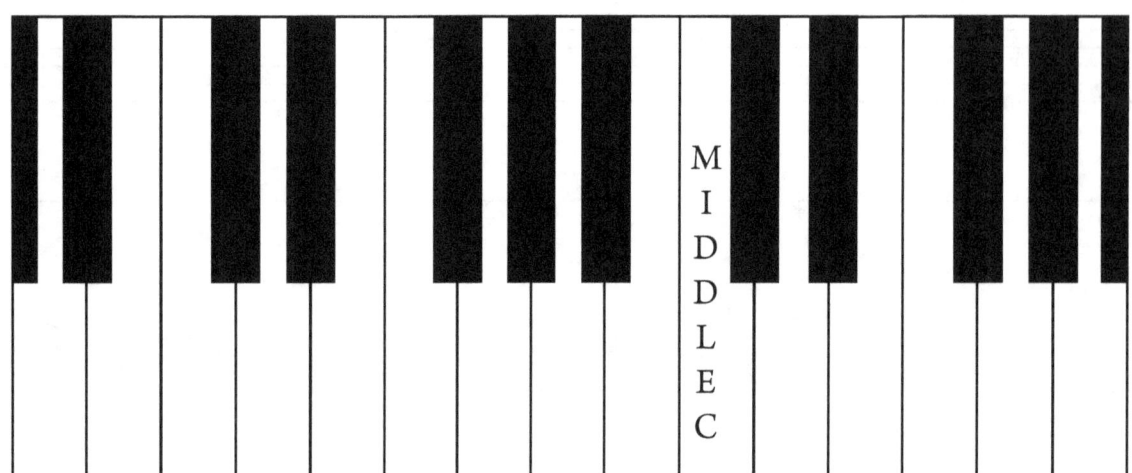

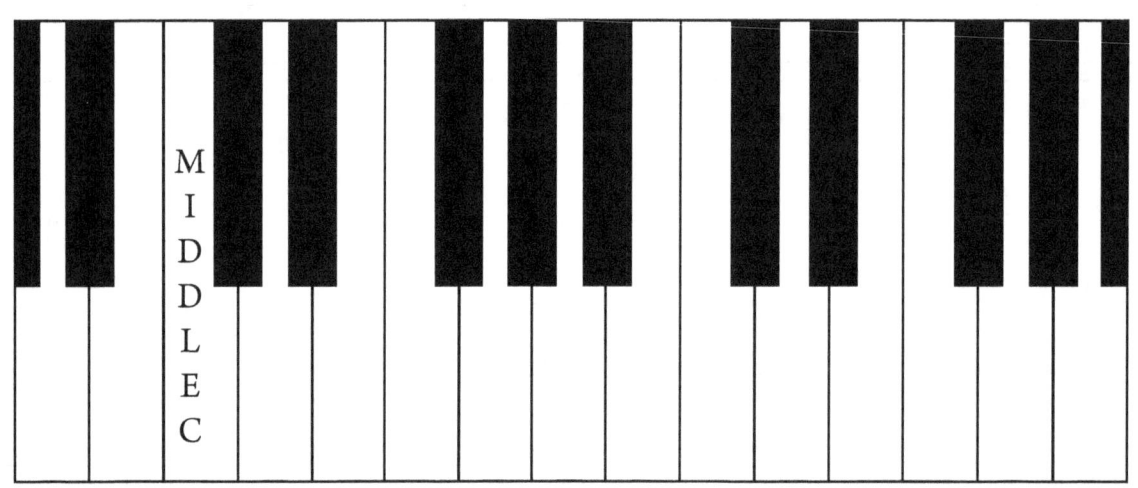

Accidentals

❶ 5. Describe the distance between the following pairs of notes as a half step or a whole step.
❷
❸

A _____ step   A _____ step   A _____ step   A _____ step

A _____ step   A _____ step   A _____ step   A _____ step

A _____ step   A _____ step   A _____ step   A _____ step

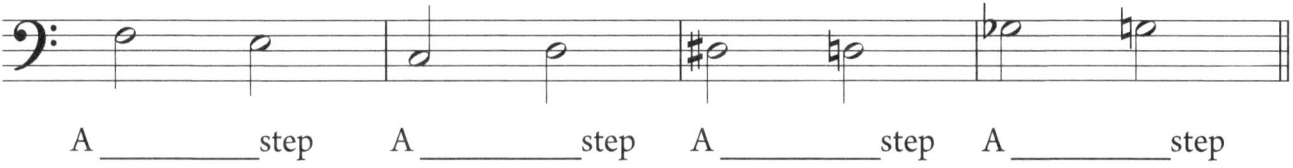

A _____ step   A _____ step   A _____ step   A _____ step

6. Write a note that is a half step above these notes.

❶❷❸ 7. Write a note that is a half step below the following notes.

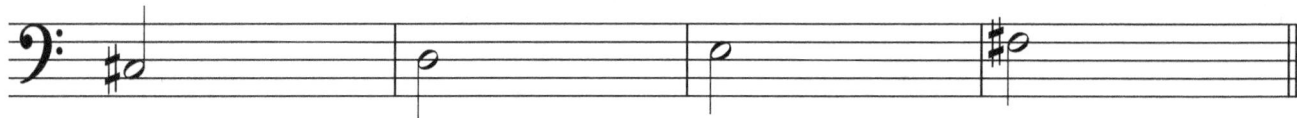

8. Write a note that is a whole step below the following notes.

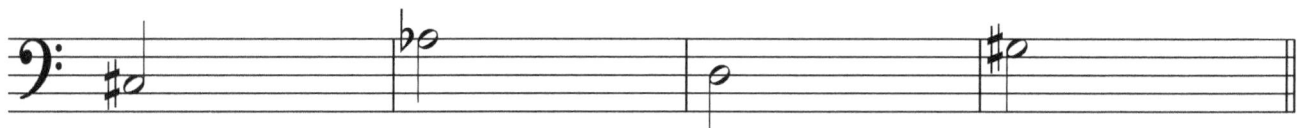

9. Write a note that is a whole step above the following notes.

❷ Half steps can also occur between two notes with different letter names. Figure 5.11 shows half steps
❸ between notes using different letter names. The note names occur in alphabetical order. For example, E♭ - F♭, F♯ - G, A - B♭, etc.

Figure 5.11

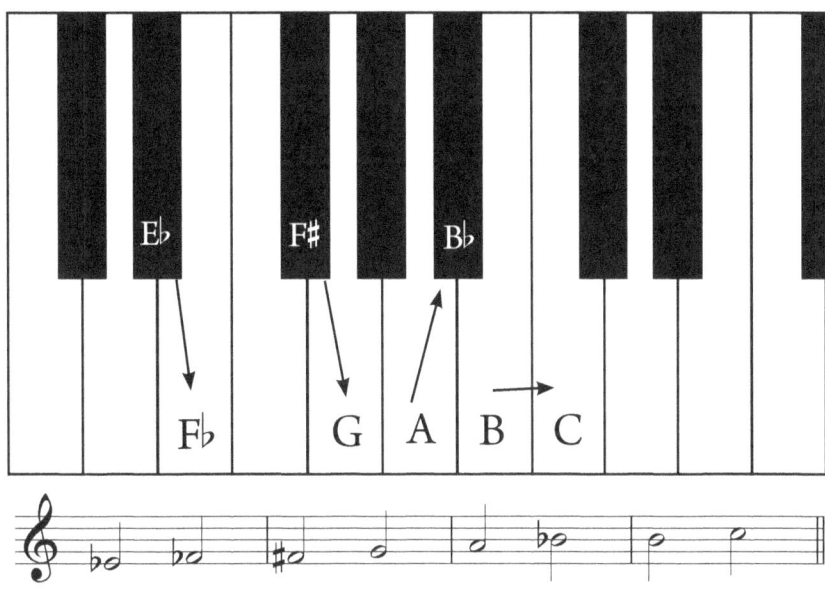

❷ 1. Write half steps above the following notes. Use notes with the different letter names.
❸

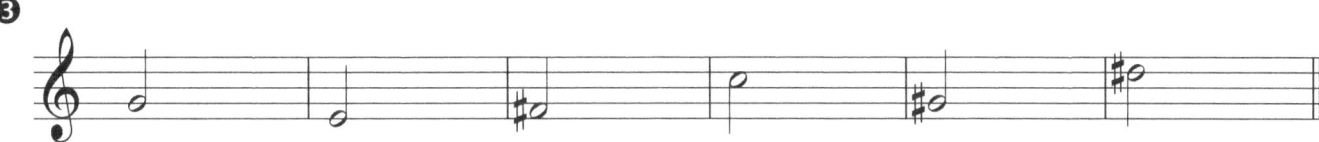

2. Write half steps below the following notes. Use notes with the different letter names.

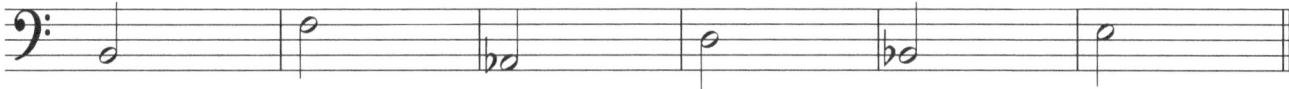

❸ Octave Transposition

An octopus has 8 legs. An octagon has 8 sides. We know from studying intervals than an *octave* is the interval that spans 8 notes.

An octave is from one letter name to the **same** letter name, up or down.

1. Write the note that is one octave above the following notes. The first one is done for you.

2. Write the note that is one octave below the following notes.

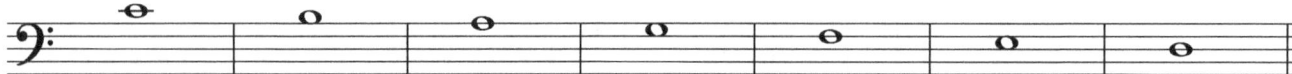

Transposition involves moving a group of notes up or down. In this level we are going to transpose by writing melodies up and down one octave in the same clef.

Figure 5.12 shows a short melody transposed up one octave in the the treble clef. The key and rhythm remain the same, but the stem direction changes.

Figure 5.12

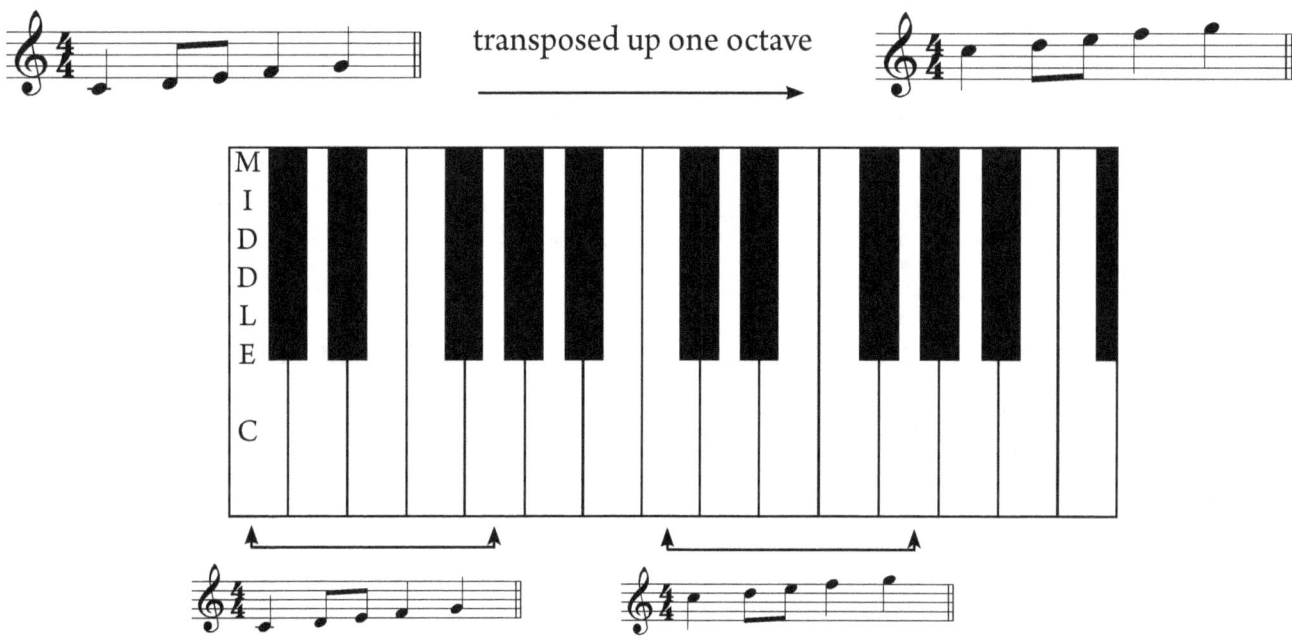

© San Marco Publications 2023   Accidentals

❸ Figure 5.13 contains a melody in G major transposed down one octave in the bass clef. The key signature, time signature, and rhythm remain the same. Every note is moved down one octave and the normal rules of stem direction are followed.

Figure 5.13

original melody   transposed down one octave in the same clef

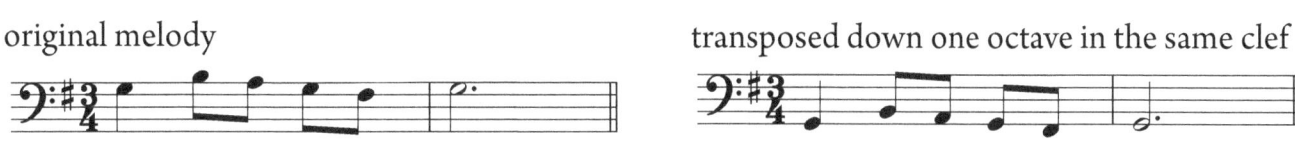

❸1. Transpose the following melody up one octave in the treble clef.

2. Transpose the following melody down one octave in the bass clef.

3. Transpose the following melody up one octave in the bass clef.

6

Intervals 1

Measuring Distance

In music, an *interval* is defined as the distance from one note to the next. Intervals are one of the building blocks in music. They are used everywhere, from scales and chords to many more complex musical things.

Intervals are expressed as numbers. For now, we will deal with the intervals from 1 to 8. There are two basic types of intervals: *harmonic* and *melodic*.

- A harmonic interval occurs when two notes are played or sung at the same time.
- A melodic interval occurs when two notes are played or sung one after the other.

Figure 6.1

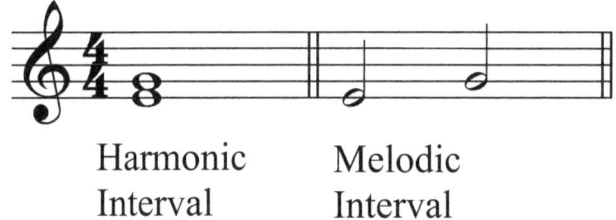

Harmonic Interval   Melodic Interval

Intervals are numbered. To determine the number of an interval, count up from the lowest note to the highest note. This is done even if the lowest note comes after the highest note.

Figure 6.2

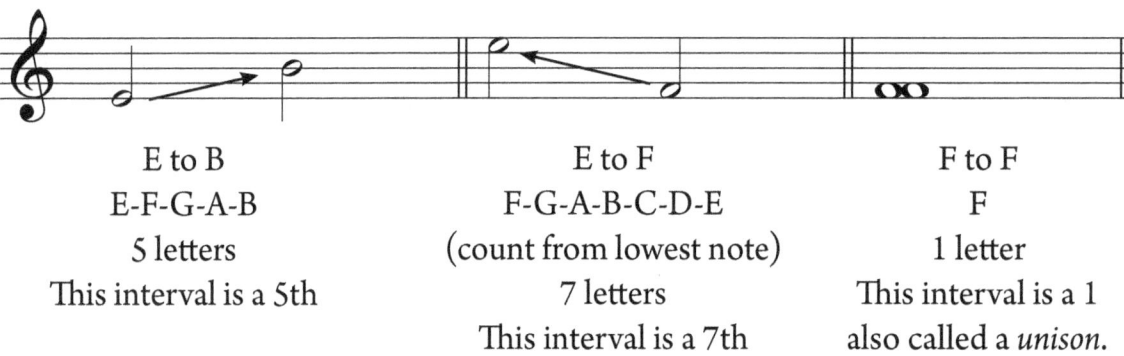

E to B   E to F   F to F
E-F-G-A-B   F-G-A-B-C-D-E   F
5 letters   (count from lowest note)   1 letter
This interval is a 5th   7 letters   This interval is a 1
    This interval is a 7th   also called a *unison*.

❶ Figure 6.3 contains all the melodic intervals up to an octave. The interval 1 is also called a *unison* and
❷ 8 is called an *octave*.
❸
Figure 6.3

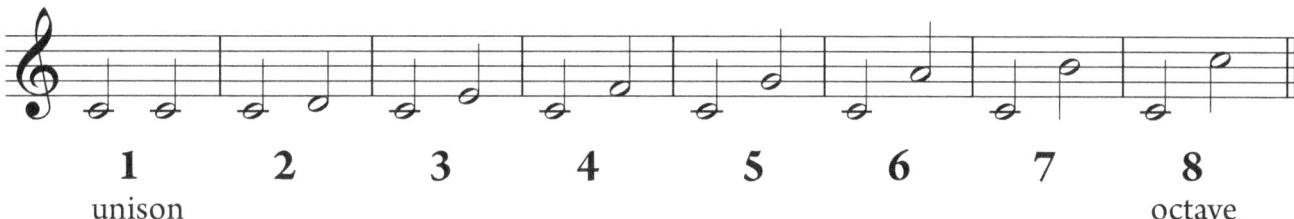

❶ 1. Write the number name of the following intervals.
❷
❸

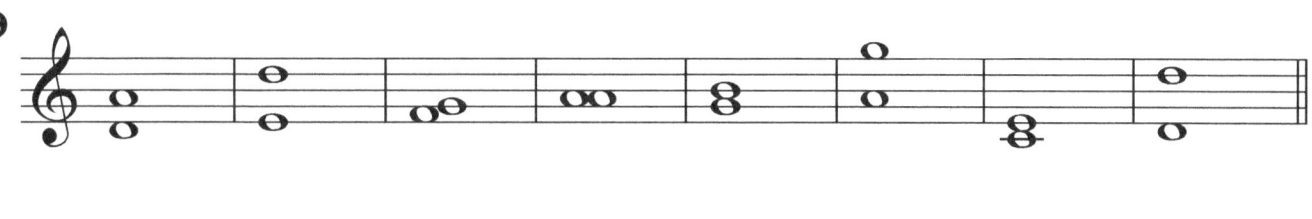

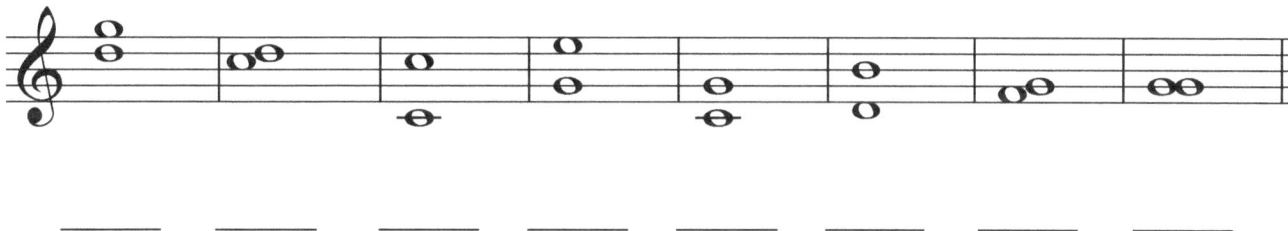

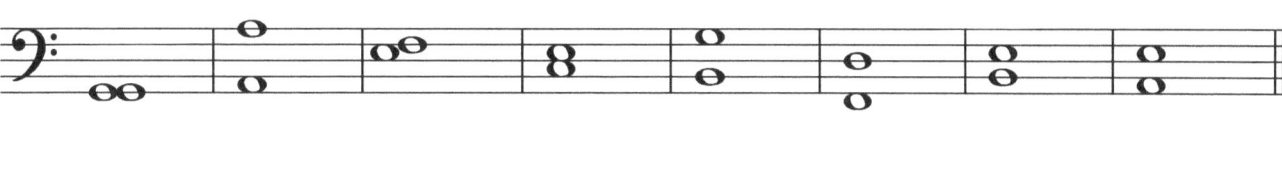

❶ 2. Write the following harmonic intervals above the given notes.
❷
❸

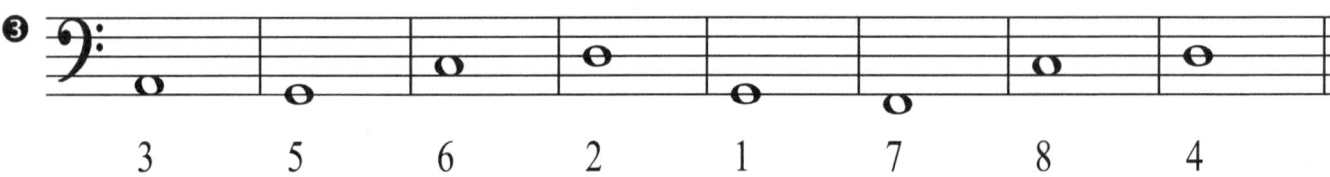

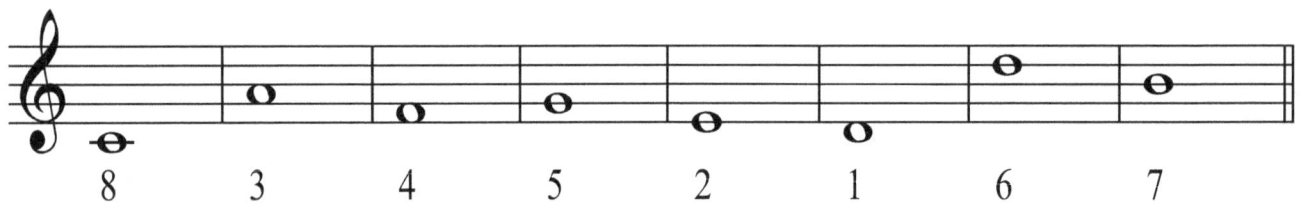

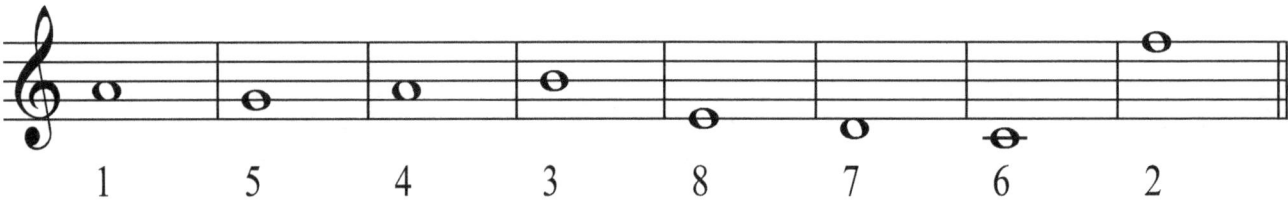

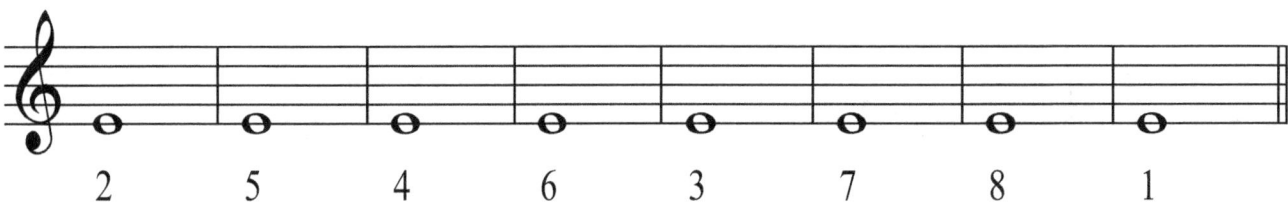

❶ 3. Write the following melodic intervals above the given notes.
❷
❸

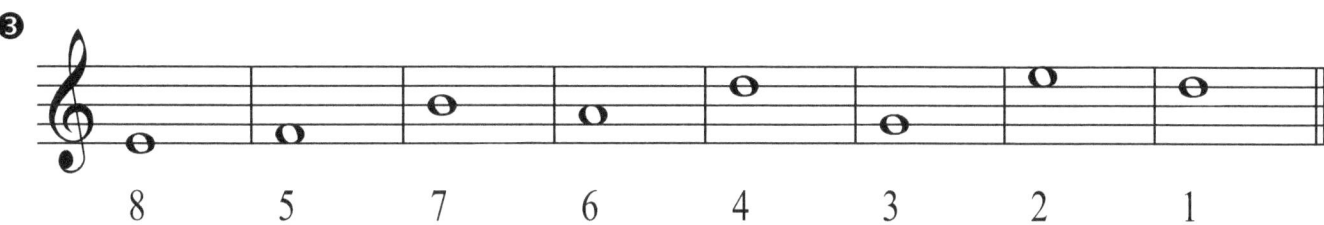

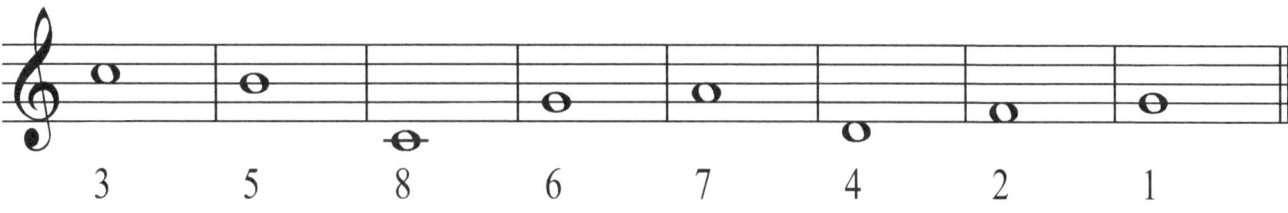

7

Major Scales

What is a scale?

Almost all music is based on a scale of some sort. Classical, country, rock, pop, hip-hop, jazz, and others are usually built in some way on some scale. The ***major scale*** is the most common scale.

A scale is a group of notes that occur in a specific order. The major scale is a series of eight notes (seven different pitches) that begin and end on the same note. The starting and ending note is called the ***tonic***. The major scale is named after the tonic. If the tonic is C, it is the C major scale. If the tonic is G, it's the G major scale. Figure 7.1 is the C major scale. It starts and ends on C and moves up every note in order. On the keyboard, it consists of all the white keys from C to C. It has seven different notes, C-D-E-F-G-A-B. The eighth note (C) is not counted as a new pitch because it is a repetition of the first note, but the major scale has eight notes in total. Each of these eight notes can be identified with a number with a small tent on top. This tent is called a caret ($\hat{1}$). When a number has a caret on top, it refers to ***scale degree***, which is just the number of the note as it occurs in the order of the scale. The first note is scale degree $\hat{1}$, the second is scale degree $\hat{2}$, etc.

Figure 7.1

Notice that the scale in Figure 8.1 goes from C to C, a distance of eight notes. This is the interval of an ***octave***. From one letter name to the next same letter name, up or down, is an octave. This scale is the C major scale, one octave, ascending.

❶❷❸ Building the Major Scale

The major scale is constructed from a specific pattern of whole steps and half steps. All major scales follow the same pattern. Remember that a half step is the smallest distance between two notes. On the piano, it is the distance from any key to the next closest key.

If we examine the C major scale again (Figure 7.2) we can see a pattern of whole and half steps that happens in all major scales. Under the scale you can see whole, whole, half, whole, whole, whole, half. This is the same order for all major scales (WWHWWWH).

The scale can also be divided into two four note sections called tetrachords. Each tetrachord is WWH with a W between the two (WWH W WWH).

Figure 7.2

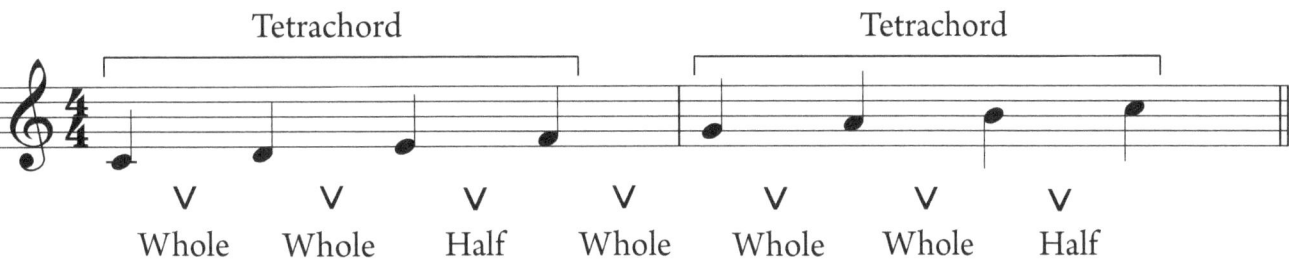

❶❷❸ 1. Mark the whole steps (W) and half steps (H) under the following scales. Above each one, label each scale degree with a number and caret. Mark the tonic note with a T.

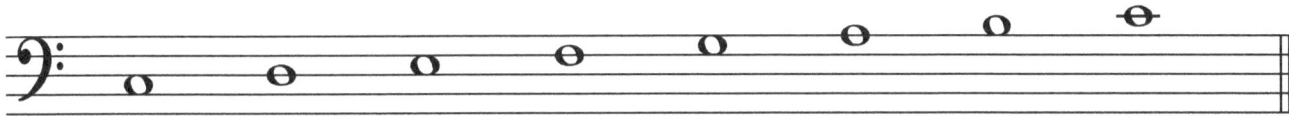

❶ Scale degree one (1̂) is called the tonic. This is the most important note of any scale. The second
❷ most important note is scale degree five (5̂). This note is called the ***dominant***. Major scales are
❸ most often written and played ascending and descending as in Figure 7.3. Here, the tonic and dominant notes are labeled with T and D.

Figure 7.3

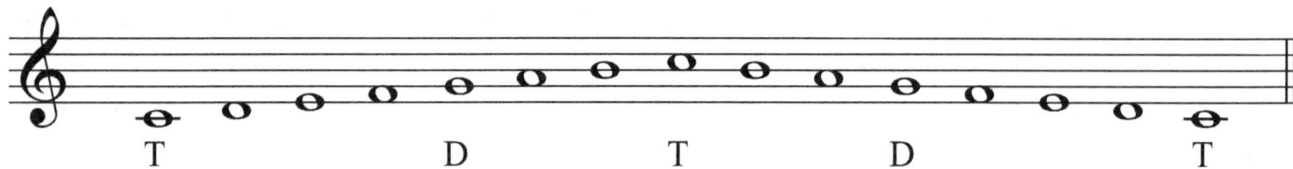

T   D   T   D   T

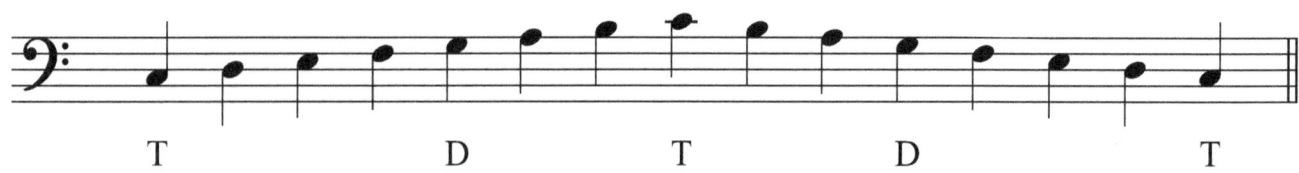

T   D   T   D   T

❶ 2. Write the C major scale ascending and descending using half notes. Mark the tonic (T) and
❷ dominant (D) notes.
❸

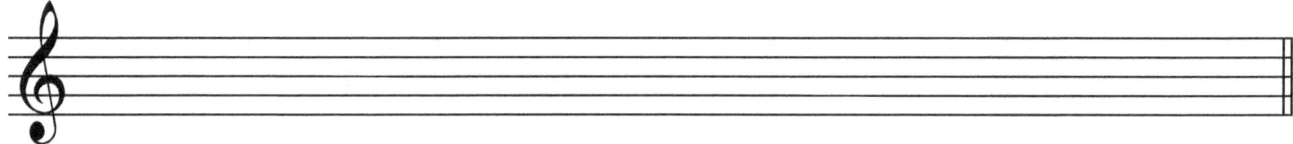

3. Write the C major scale ascending and descending using quarter notes. Mark the tonic (T) and dominant (D) notes.

Major Scales

The G Major Scale

Using the same pattern of whole and half steps we can write major scales starting on any note. If we write a major scale starting on G, we must alter one note to get the correct pattern of whole and half steps (WWHWWWH). Figure 7.4 shows that an F♯ is necessary to get the correct pattern of whole and half steps. We need an F♯ between $\hat{7}$ and $\hat{8}$ to have a half step, which also gives us the whole step we need between $\hat{6}$ and $\hat{7}$. The G major scale contains one sharp, F♯.

Figure 7.4

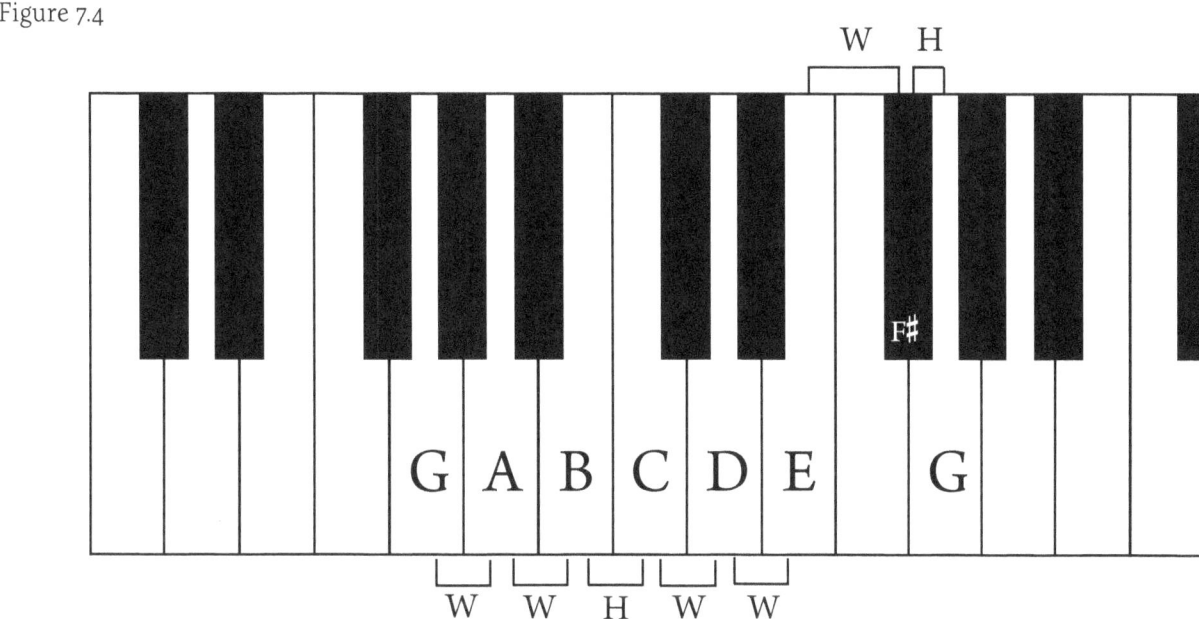

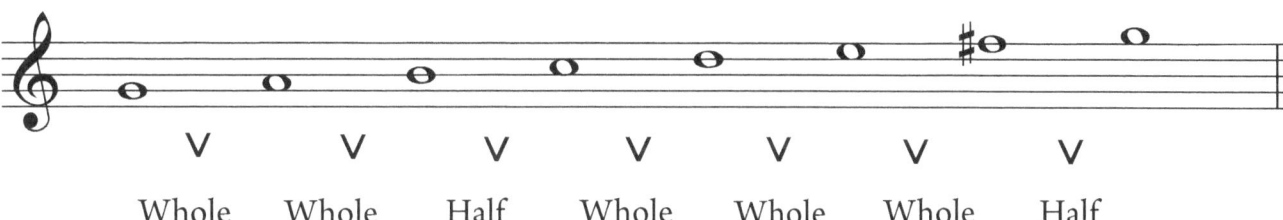

4. Write the G major scale ascending and descending using whole notes. Mark the tonic (T) and dominant (D) notes.

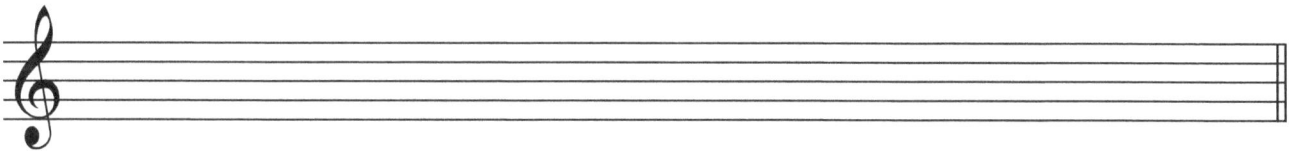

The F Major Scale

For the F major scale, a B♭ is required to have a half step between $\hat{3}$ and $\hat{4}$. The B♭ also creates the required whole step between $\hat{4}$ and $\hat{5}$. E to F is a natural half step between $\hat{7}$ and $\hat{8}$ so they do not need to be altered. This is shown in Figure 7.5. The F major scale has one flat, B♭.

Figure 7.5

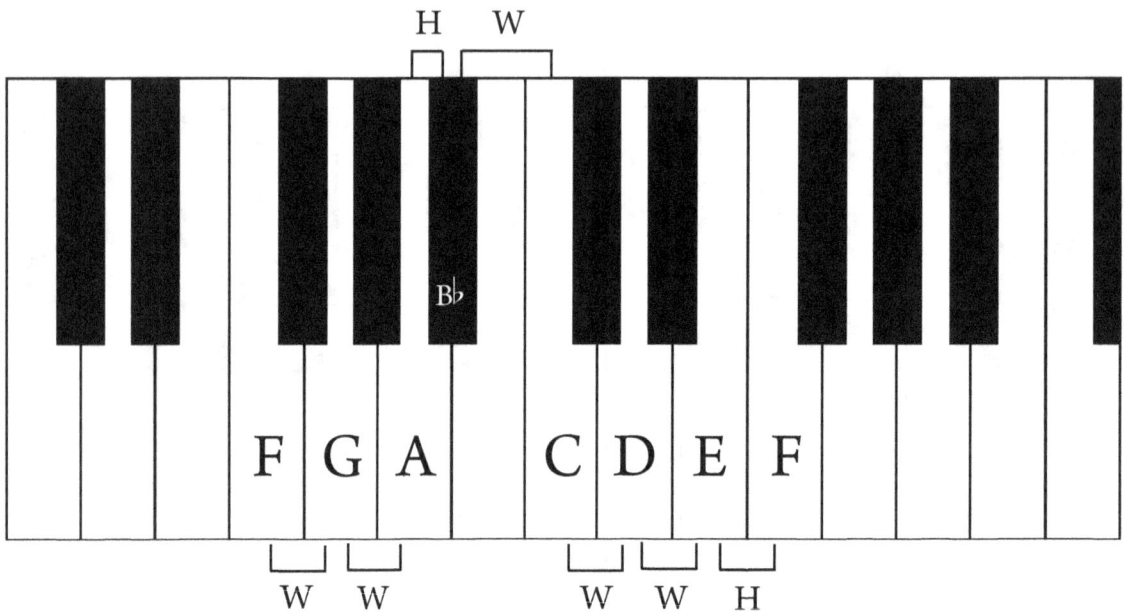

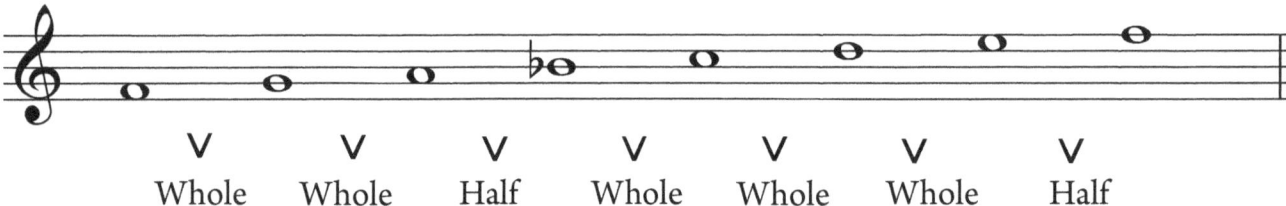

5. Write the F major scale ascending and descending using whole notes. Mark the tonic (T) and dominant (D) notes.

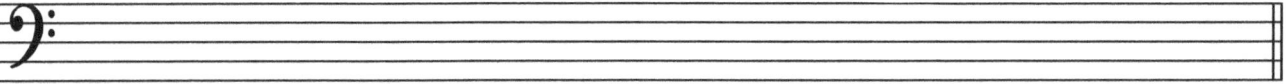

6. Write the following scales ascending and descending according to the instructions.

C major in whole notes

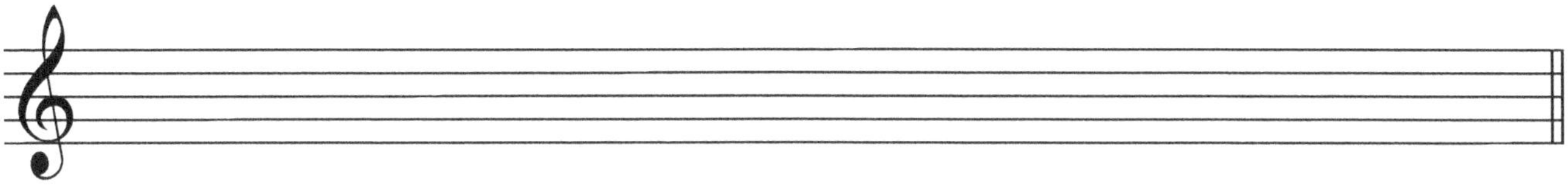

F major in quarter notes

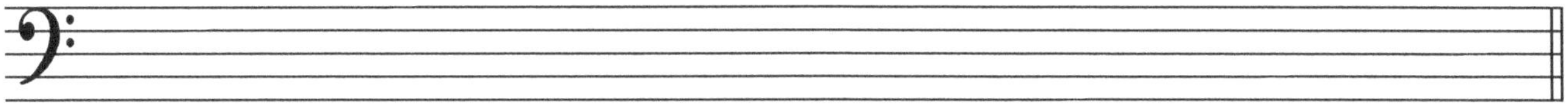

G major in whole notes

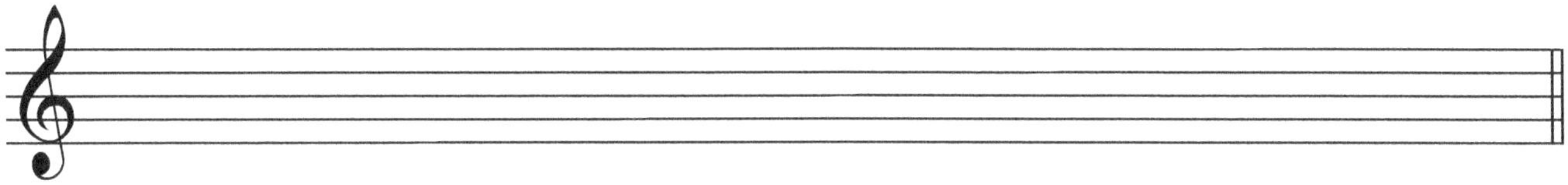

C major in half notes

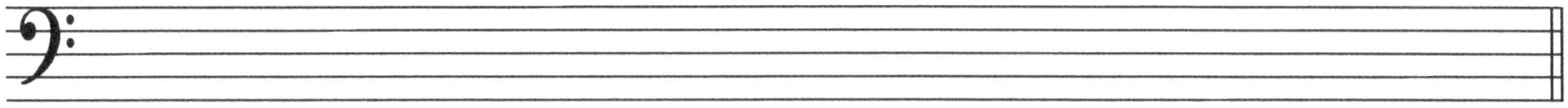

F major in whole notes

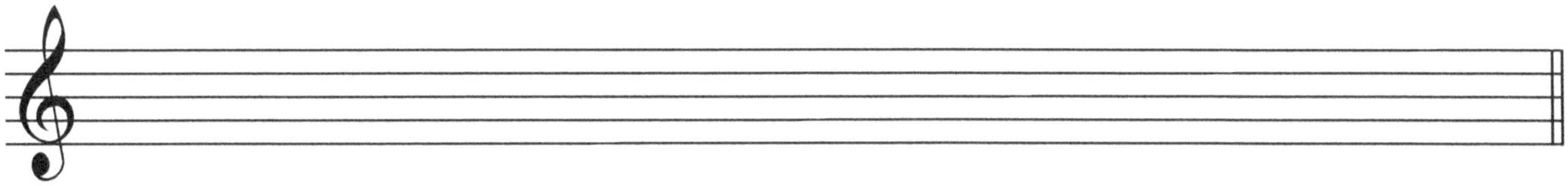

7. The following notes are all from the scale of C major. Label each with a scale degree number (1̂, 2̂, 3̂, etc) above each note. Label the tonic (T) and dominant (D) notes.

8. The following notes are all from the scale of F major. Label each with a scale degree number (1̂, 2̂, 3̂, etc) above each note. Label the tonic (T) and dominant (D) notes.

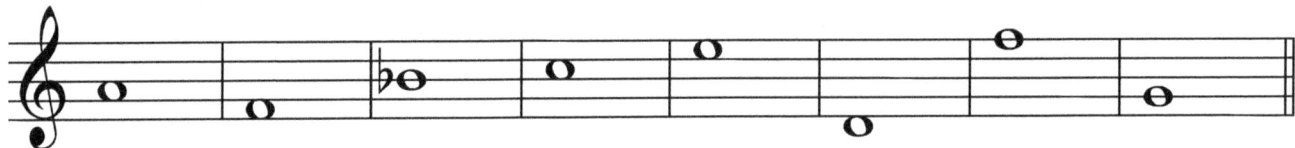

9. The following notes are all from the scale of G major. Label each with a scale degree number (1̂, 2̂, 3̂, etc) above each note. Label the tonic (T) and dominant (D) notes.

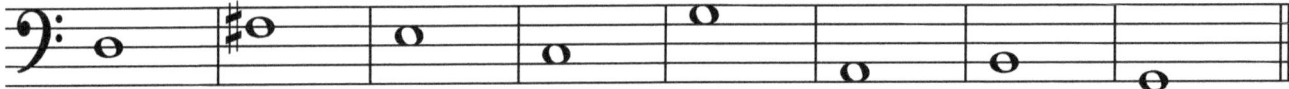

Key Signatures

The ***key signature*** is an essential element in the organization of music. Instead of writing all the accidentals throughout a piece of music, composers place them all at the beginning of the staff. The key signature contains the sharps and flats that occur in a piece of music. It tells us the scale the music is based on, and usually the starting and ending notes. It gives us the flats or sharps in a composition. Key signatures never contain both sharps and flats. They will contain all sharps or all flats or nothing at all.

When writing scales in the last lesson, we raised or lowered certain notes with accidentals to get the correct pattern of whole and half steps. Every key signature has the same name as the scale. The key of G major will have the same accidentals as the G major scale (F♯). The key of F major will have the same accidentals as the F major scale (B♭).

The key signature at the beginning of a piece applies to the entire composition unless the composer changes it or adds accidentals. Figure 7.6 shows the F major scale first with accidentals, and then with a key signature. The key signature of F major is one flat (B♭). When it is placed at the beginning of the music there is no need to add B♭'s to the music. The key signature makes all the Bs flat automatically.

Figure 7.6

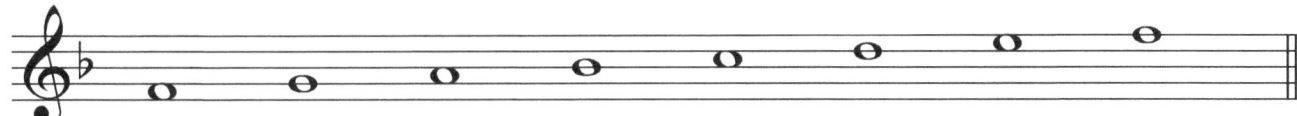

❶ The accidentals for a key signature are always placed in the same place on the staff. Figure 7.7 shows
❷ where they are put on each staff.
❸ In G major the F♯ is placed on the fifth line in the treble staff and on the fourth line in the bass staff. In F major the B♭ is placed on the third line in the treble staff and on the second line in the bass staff.

Figure 7.7

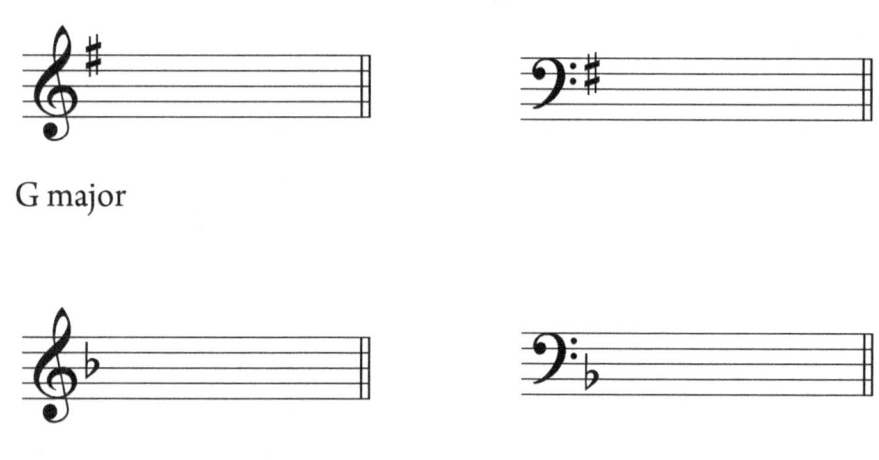

G major

F major

1. Write the following scales in whole notes ascending and descending using a key signature.

F major

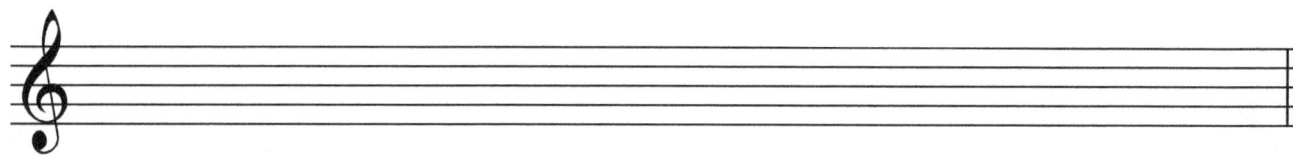

G major

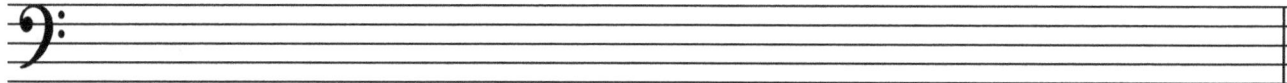

G major

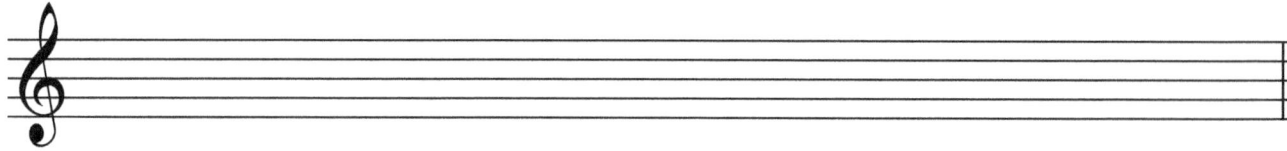

F major

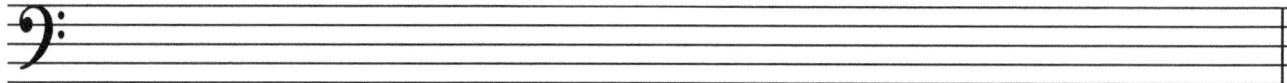

Key Signatures on the Grand Staff

Figure 7.8 contains the key signatures of F major and G major on the grand staff. The accidentals are always put in the same place in the key signature on the grand staff. Notice that the key signature comes between the clef and the time signature.

Figure 7.8

C major   F major   G major

1. Write the following scales in each clef of the grand staff using key signatures.

F major in half notes

G major in quarter notes

❶ A key signature identifies a piece of music's 'home base.' The music we are studying is called ***tonal***
❷ ***music***. In tonal music, the first note of the scale, the tonic, is the most important and central tone.
❸ When a piece of music is based on the F major scale, it has a key signature of one flat (B♭) and is said to be *in the key of F major*. F is the most important note, and often (but not always) the piece will begin and end on F. Starting and ending on F establishes the 'home base.'

The melody in Figure 7.9 is in the key of G major. It uses the key signature of G major (F♯) and begins and ends on G, the tonic of G major.

Figure 7.9

G major

1. Name the keys of the following melodies.

Key:_____

Key:_____

Key:_____

Key:_____

❷
❸ 10. Name the scale degree ($\hat{1}$, $\hat{2}$, $\hat{3}$, etc.) of the notes marked with * in each of the following. The first answer is shown.

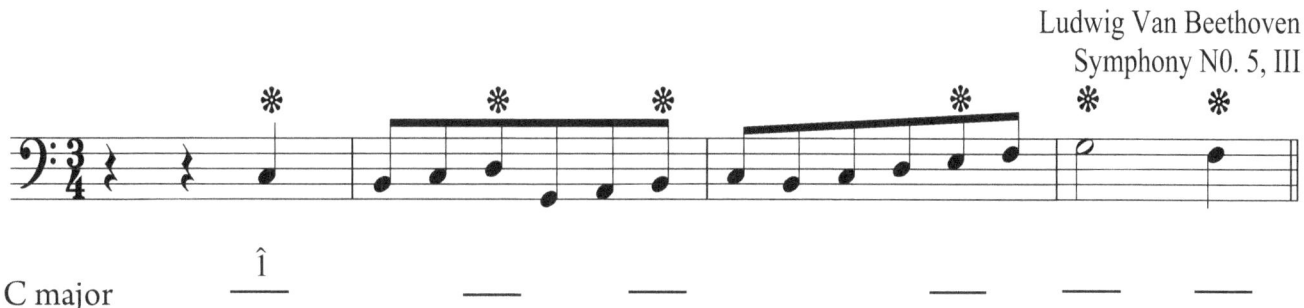

C major $\hat{1}$

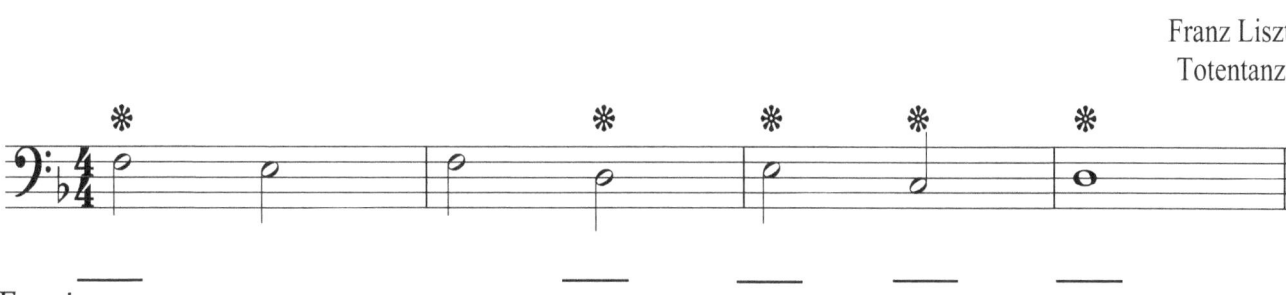

F major

G major

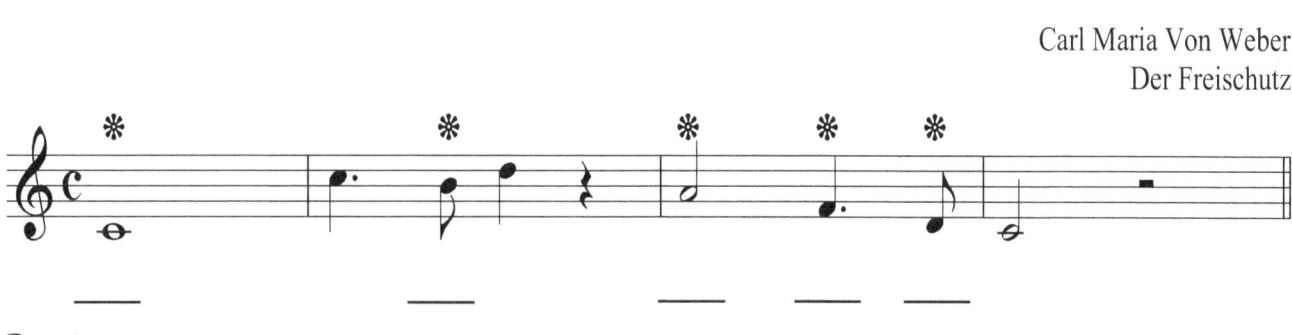

C major

Music Terms

Terms Relating to Tempo

The word **tempo** comes from the Latin *tempus* which means time. Words that deal with tempo refer to how fast or slow we play music. Study the following Italian terms.

a tempo   return to the previous tempo

allegretto   fairly fast, a little slower than allegro

presto   very fast

rallentando, rall.   slowing down

Tempo Terms Review

5. The following terms are from Level 1. Draw lines to match the correct term with its meaning.

tempo   slowing down gradually

lento   fast

andante   at a moderate tempo

moderato   moderaltely slow; at a walking pace

allegro   slow

ritardando, rit   speed at which music is performed

© San Marco Publications 2023

Major Scales

❸ Here are the key signatures on the grand staff for keys up to two sharps and flats.

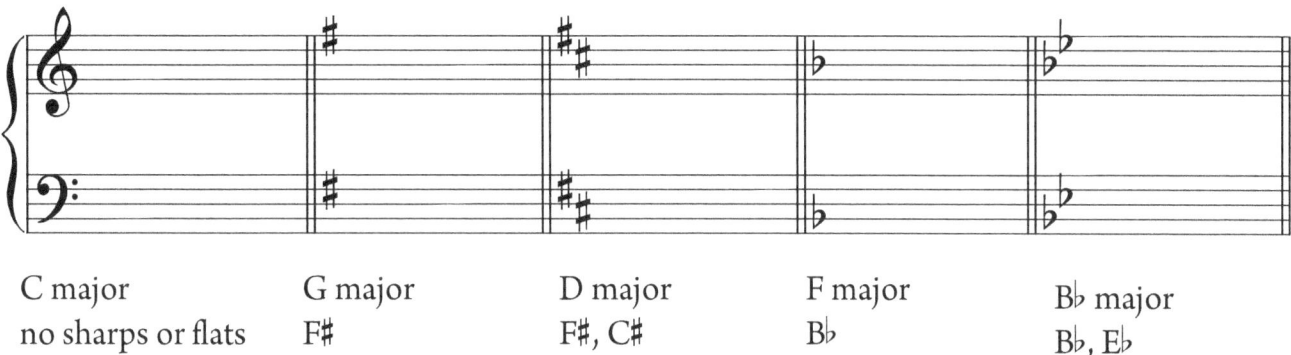

C major — no sharps or flats
G major — F#
D major — F#, C#
F major — B♭
B♭ major — B♭, E♭

1. Write the following key signatures on the grand staff.

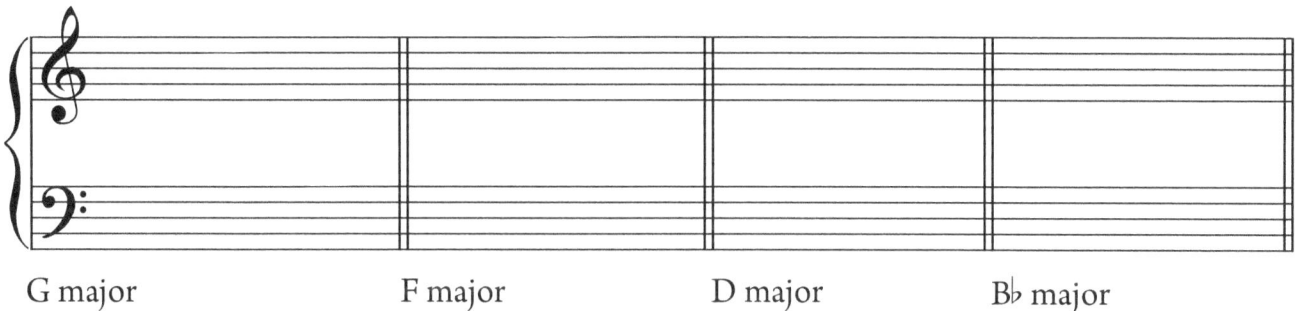

G major   F major   D major   B♭ major

Each scale can be labelled with a scale degree ($\hat{1}$, $\hat{2}$, $\hat{3}$, etc.). There are also technical names for the scale degrees. $\hat{1}$ is the tonic, $\hat{4}$ is the subdominant and $\hat{5}$ is the dominant. Scale degree $\hat{7}$ is known as the leading tone. This is because it is a half step away from, and leads to the tonic. Play a major scale and stop on the leading tone. Listen to the pull the leading tone has to the tonic note.

Figure 7.10

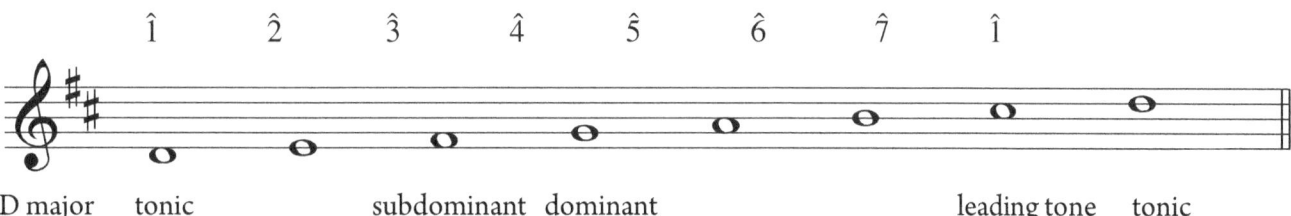

D major   tonic   subdominant   dominant   leading tone   tonic

❸ 1. Write the following scales ascending and descending using a key signature for each. Label the leading tone (LT).

D major in half notes

F major in quarter notes

G major in single sixteenth notes

C major in whole notes

B♭ major in dotted half notes

Major Scales

❸ 2. Add clefs and key signatures to complete the following major scales. Mark the half steps with a slur and label the tonic (T), dominant (D), and leading tones (LT).

B♭ major

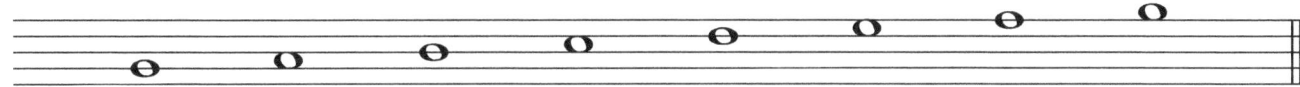

D major

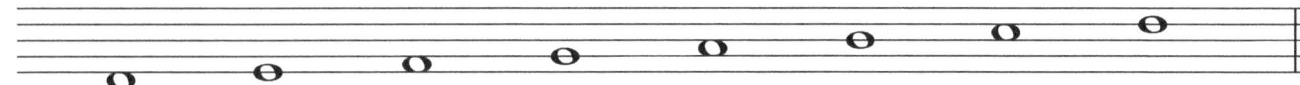

F major

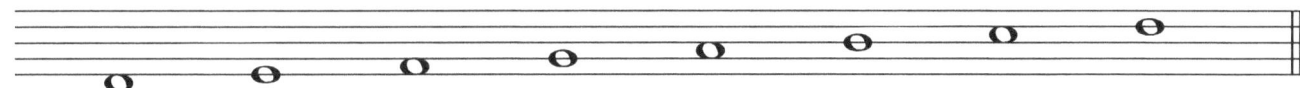

G major

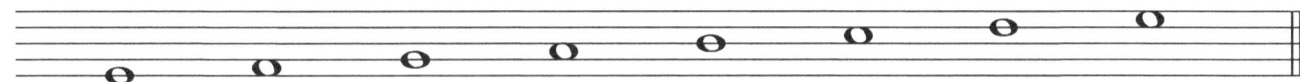

C major

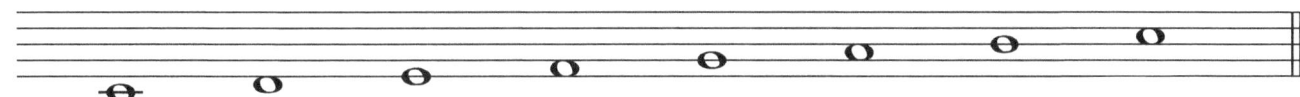

❸ 3. Identify the following major key signatures.

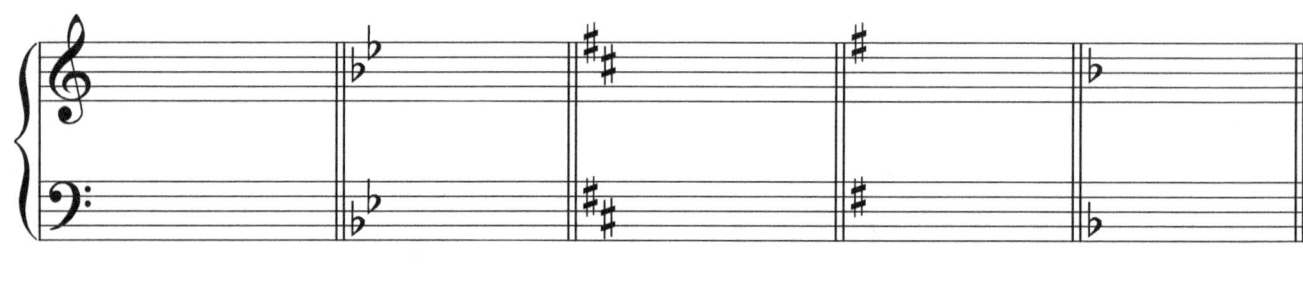

Key: _____ _____ _____ _____ _____

4. Write the following scales ascending and descending in whole notes using accidentals instead of a key signature.

The major scale with 2 flats

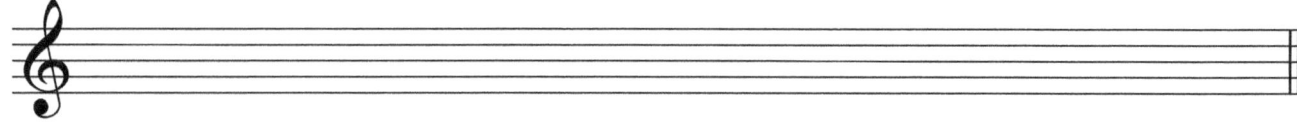

key:

The major scale with 1 sharp

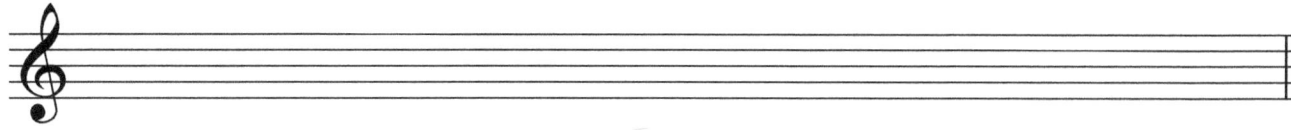

key:

The major scale with 1 flat

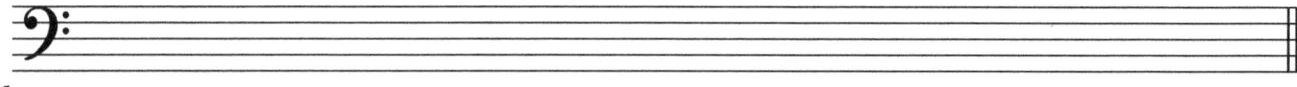

key:

The major scale with 2 sharps

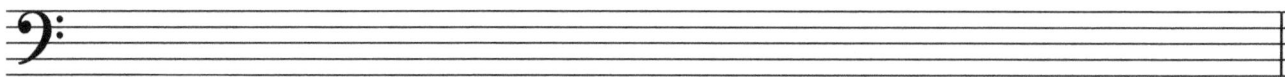

key:

❸5. Answer the following questions.

   a. Name the leading tone of the F major scale: _____

   b. Name the dominant of the G major scale: _____

   c. Name the subdominant of the B♭ major scale: _____

   d. Name the tonic of the D major scale: _____

   e. Name the leading tone of the C major scale: _____

❸6. Write the following scales ascending and descending in half notes using a key signature for each.

The major scale with C♯ as the leading tone

The major scale with C as the dominant

The major scale with C as the subdominant

8

Minor Scales

The Natural Minor Scale

A major scale evokes a particular color or character in sound. A ***minor scale*** has a different color or character. Some might say it has a sadder or darker sound, but that is a matter of opinion. The minor scale is another essential scale in music, and it occurs frequently.

There are three types of minor scales. We will begin by studying the ***natural minor scale***. The natural minor scale has a specific pattern of whole and half steps. This scale is constructed using the pattern WHWWHWW. The half steps occur between $\hat{2}$ and $\hat{3}$ and $\hat{5}$ and $\hat{6}$. Figure 8.1 contains the A natural minor scale, using this interval pattern. Using this pattern you can construct a natural minor scale on any note. The key is written as 'A minor.'

Figure 8.1

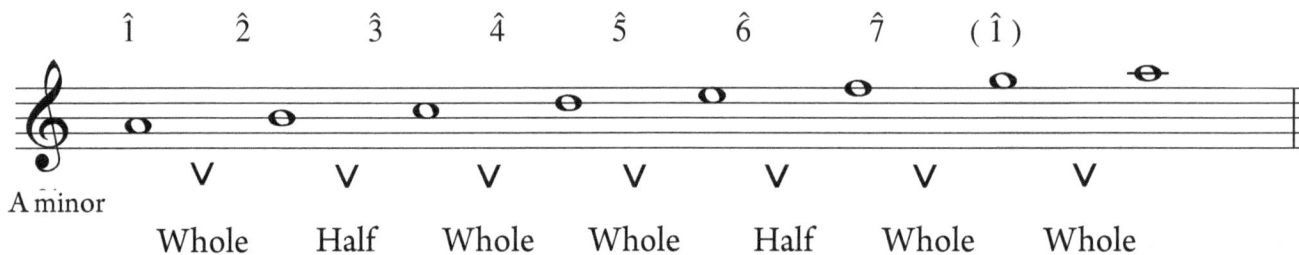

❶
❷ The Origin of the Minor Scale
❸

Major and minor scales are known as ***modes***. A mode is an ancient scale. If you play a major scale starting and ending on a different note than the tonic you get a mode. In fact, a minor scale lives inside a major scale. The minor scale can be found by playing the major scale from the 6th note to the 6th note.

Relative Minor Keys

Figure 8.2 is the C major scale. It is C major because of the arrangement of whole and half steps and because it starts and ends on C. C is the tonic, which is the most important note in any key. A composition in C major is all about C, and is usually centered around the note C. The tonic is home base and a piece of music sounds complete when it ends on the tonic.

Figure 8.2

C major

If you play a major scale from the 6th note to the 6th note you get a natural minor scale. The C major scale played from A to A, produces the A natural minor scale (Figure 8.3). All of the notes in A natural minor come from the C major scale. A minor is the ***relative minor*** of C major. A minor and C major are related by key signature. They each have the same number of flats or sharps. C major's relative minor is A minor, and A minor's relative major is C major. Both keys have no sharps or flats in their key signature.

Figure 8.3

A natural minor

❶❷❸ The A Natural Minor Scale

The A natural minor scale is the C major scale played from scale degree $\hat{6}$ (A) to $\hat{6}$ (A). Since C major and A minor share the same key signature, there are no sharps or flats in the A natural minor scale.

Figure 8.4

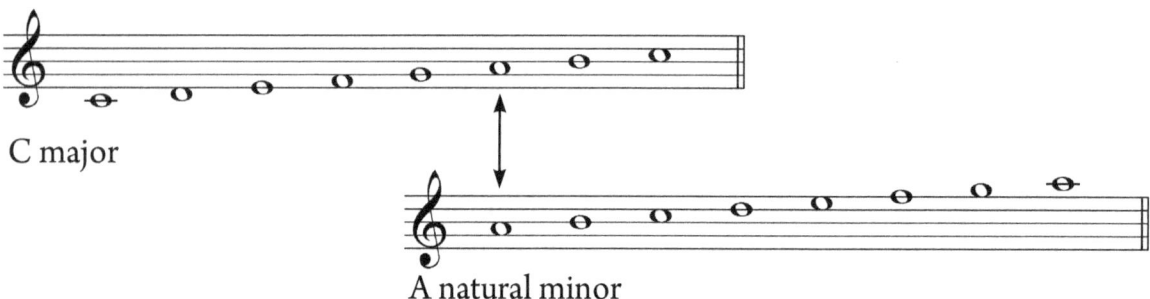

The tonic of A natural minor is A ($\hat{1}$).
The dominant of A natural minor is E ($\hat{5}$).

Figure 8.5

A natural minor scale

❶1. Write the following scales ascending and descending. Mark the tonic (T) and dominant (D)
❷ notes.
❸

A natural minor in half notes

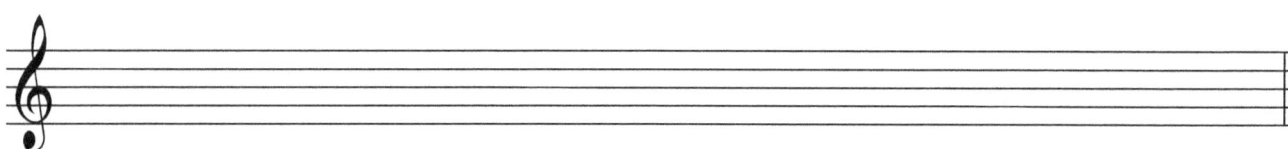

A natural minor in quarter notes

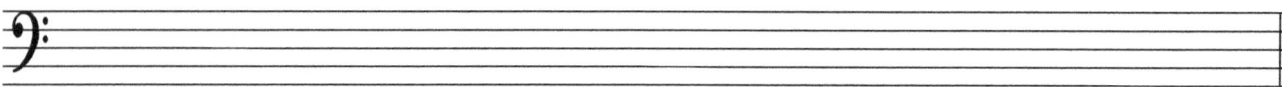

❷ If you play the G major scale from its 6th note (E to E), you get its relative minor, E natural minor.
❸ Figure 8.6 shows these two scales using accidentals. They can also be written with the key signature of one sharp (F♯). They are related because they each have an F♯ in their key signatures.

Figure 8.6

G major

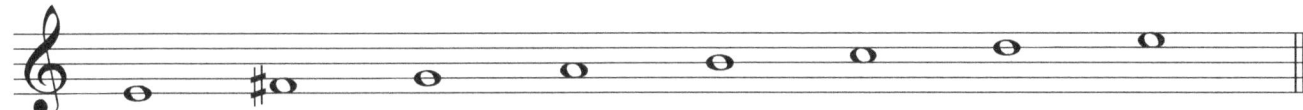

E natural minor

❷ Figure 8.7 contains the F major scale and its relative minor, D minor. The 6th note of F major is D. These examples
❸ use the key signature (B♭). The key signature is the same for both scales because they are relatives.

Figure 8.7

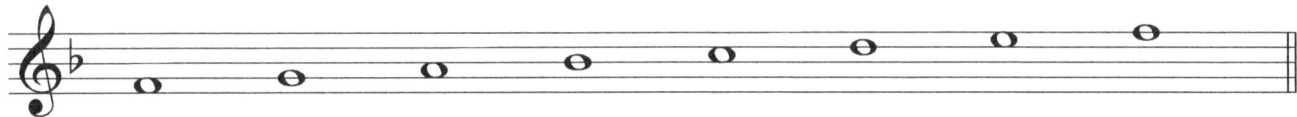

F major

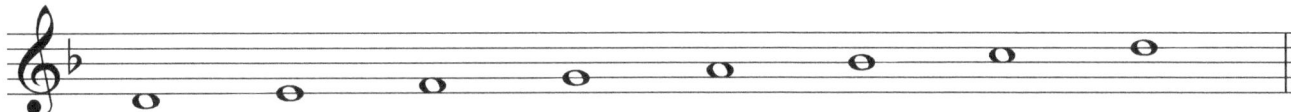

D natural minor

❷ 1. Name the relative minors of the following major keys.
❸

        C major   _____

        G major   _____

        F major   _____

❷ 2. Write the following scales ascending and descending using a key signature.
❸   Mark the tonic (T) and the subdominant notes (SD).

E natural minor in half notes

D natural minor in whole notes

A natural minor in quarter notes

E natural minor in dotted quarter notes

Minor Scales

The Harmonic Minor Scale

The *harmonic minor scale* is the most common minor scale. It is a slightly altered version of the natural minor scale. In the harmonic minor scale, $\hat{7}$ is raised one half step. The name harmonic comes from the way the scale is used. This version of the scale is required to get the music correct when writing chords. A half step is needed between $\hat{7}$ and $\hat{8}$ to create certain chord progressions in music. When $\hat{7}$ is a half step away from the tonic ($\hat{8}$), it is called the **leading tone** because it leads our ear to the tonic.

In the natural minor scale where $\hat{7}$ is not raised, and is a whole step away from the tonic, it is called the *subtonic*. When $\hat{7}$ is a whole step away it does not sound like it is leading to the tonic, so it is not called the leading tone. In minor keys we have two names for $\hat{7}$. When it is raised, it is called the **leading tone**. When it is not raised it is called the **subtonic**.

The harmonic minor uses the same key signature as the natural minor (the relative major), but there is an accidental for raised $\hat{7}$. Figure 8.8 contains the A natural minor scale and the A harmonic minor scale. A minor's relative major is C major so there are no sharps or flats in the key signature. The harmonic minor is simply the natural minor with $\hat{7}$ raised one half step. $\hat{7}$ is G and we use a sharp to raise it one half step to G♯. In the harmonic minor scale there are three half steps. They occur between $\hat{2}$ and $\hat{3}$, $\hat{5}$ and $\hat{6}$ and $\hat{7}$ and $\hat{8}$.

Figure 8.8

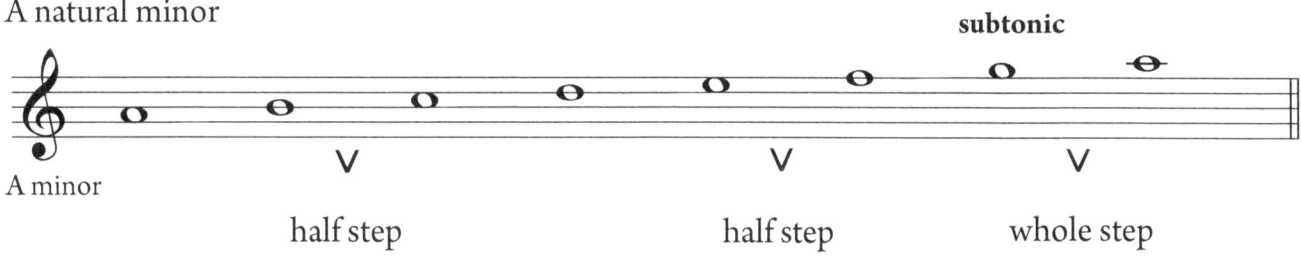

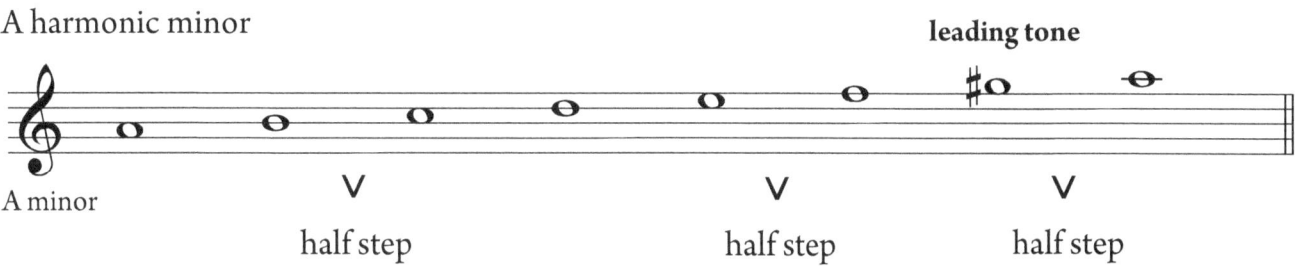

❷ The E harmonic minor scale uses the same key signature as its relative major, G major, and raised
❸ $\hat{7}$ is D♯. In Figure 8.9, for demonstration purposes, the D♯ is written ascending and descending but this is not necessary since the D remains sharp within the same measure.

Figure 8.9

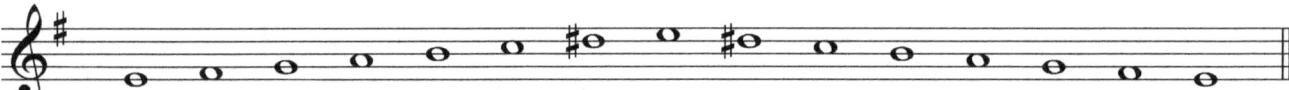

E harmonic minor

The D harmonic minor scale uses the same key signature as its relative major, F major, and includes raised $\hat{7}$, C♯.

Figure 8.10

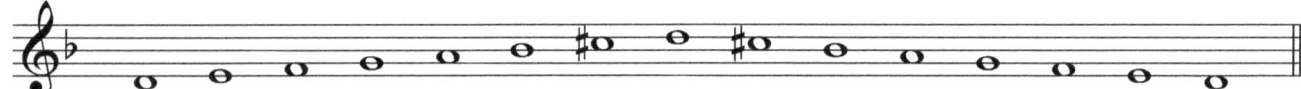

D harmonic minor

❷ 1. Using the correct key signature write the following harmonic minor scales in whole notes. Write them in
❸ both clefs on the grand staves. The first one has been started for you.

A harmonic minor

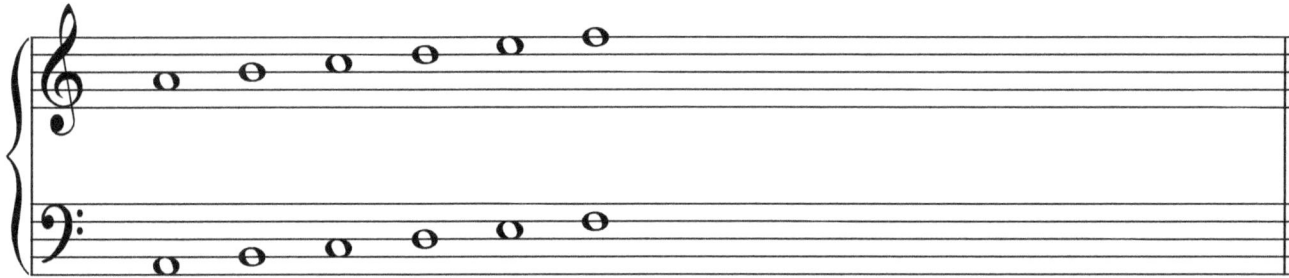

D harmonic minor

Minor Scales

❷ 2. Add clefs and accidentals to create the following scales. Label the tonic (T), subtonic (ST) and
❸   leading tones (LT).

A harmonic minor

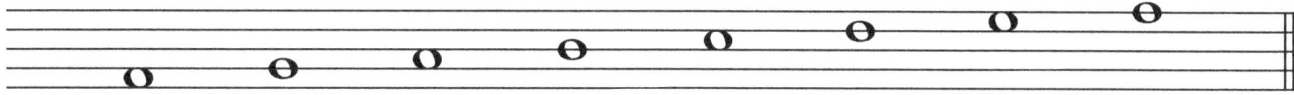

E natural minor

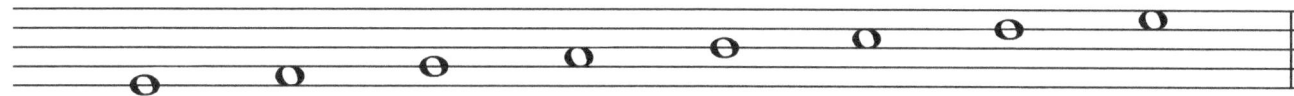

D natural minor

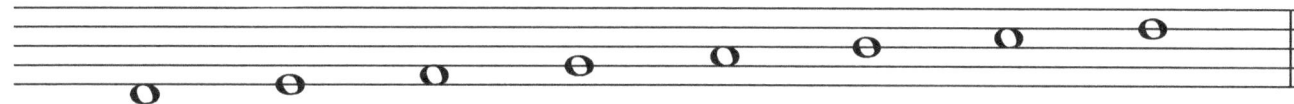

E harmonic minor

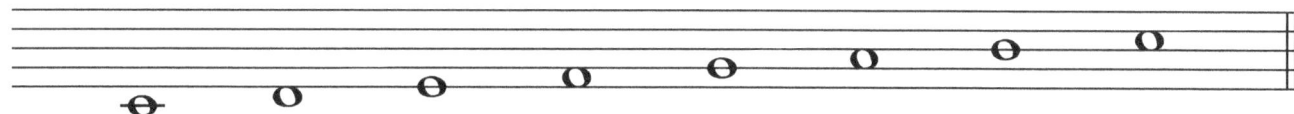

D harmonic minor

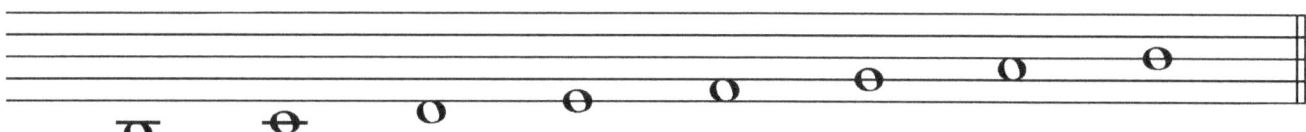

❷ ❸ 3. Using the given rhythms, write the minor scales as named below.

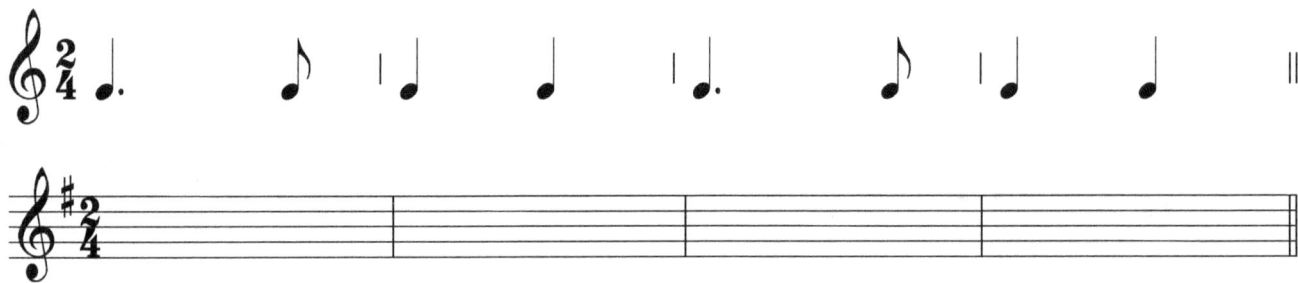

E minor harmonic ascending

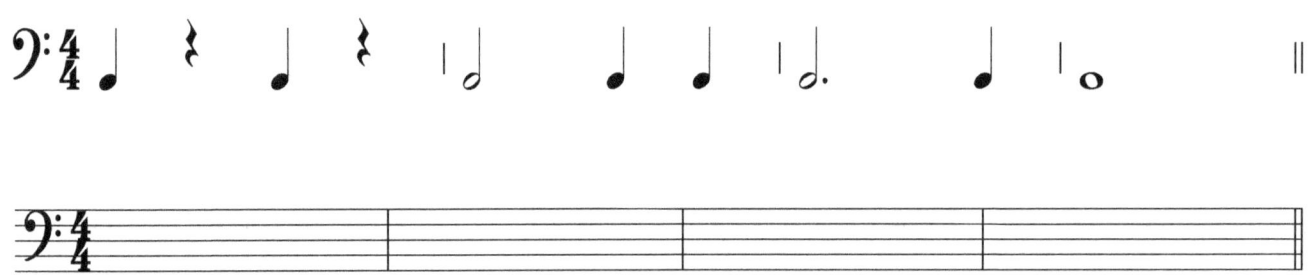

A minor harmonic decending

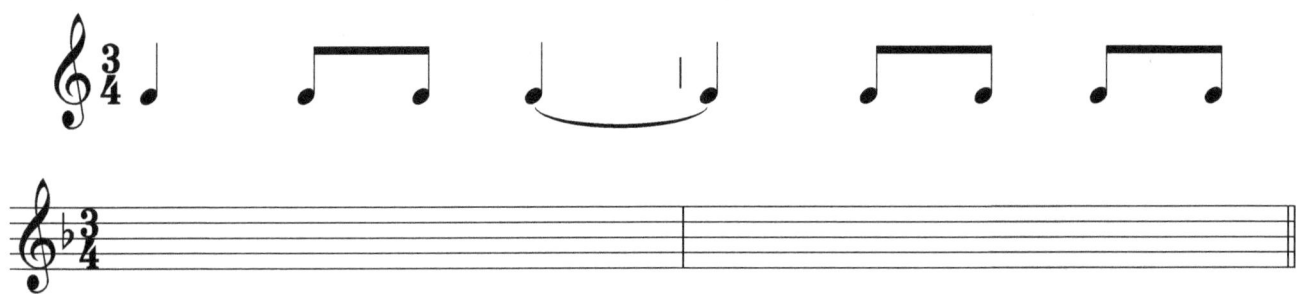

D minor harmonic asecending

Relative Minor Keys Review

Every major key has a relative minor. They are related because they share the same key signature. C major and A minor have no sharps or flats. C major is the relative major of A minor and vice versa.

To determine a minor key signature:

1. Name the major key.

2. Count up six notes (or down three) to get the relative minor key.

The 6th note of the D major scale is B. B minor has the same key signature as D major, two sharps, F♯ and C♯. Every key signature reflects two keys, one major and one minor.

Figure 8.11

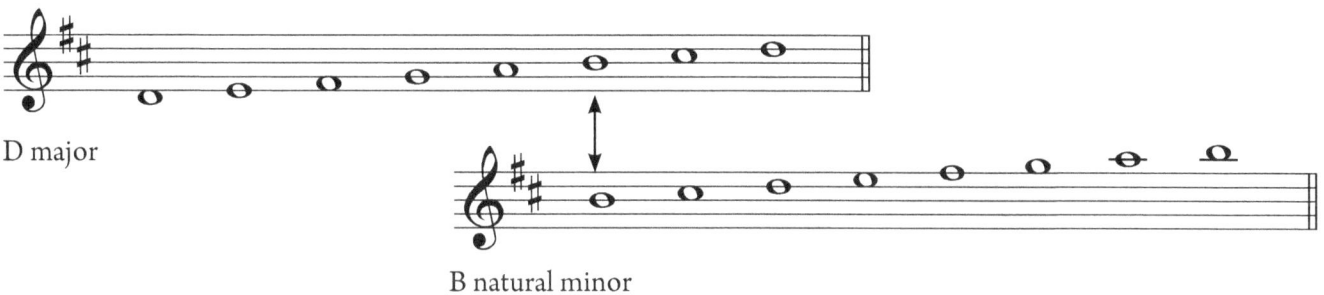

Figure 8.12 contains the relative major and minor keys up to two sharps and flats.

Figure 8.12

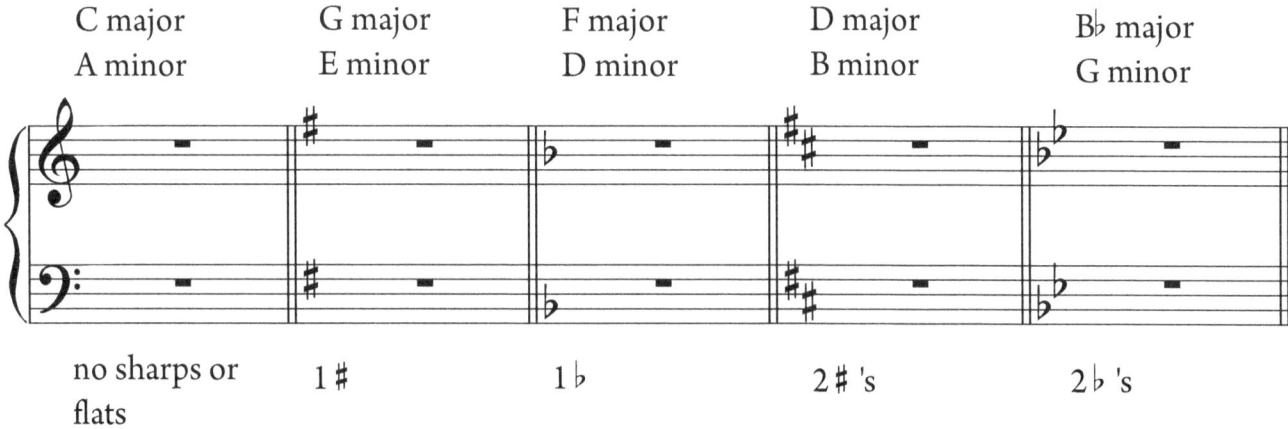

❸ 1. Name the following relative major and minor keys for the following.

D major _____   B minor _____

E minor _____   A minor _____

C major _____   G major _____

F major _____   D minor _____

❸ 2. Write the following natural minor scales ascending and descending in whole notes using a key signature. Mark the half steps with a slur.

B harmonic minor

G harmonic minor

D natural minor

Minor Scales

The Melodic Minor Scale

The *melodic minor scale* is based on the natural minor scale but contains altered notes. This scale is different ascending than it is descending.

On the way up, scale degrees $\hat{6}$ and $\hat{7}$ are raised one half step, and on the way down, they are lowered one half step. The whole point of this scale is to smooth out the space between $\hat{6}$ and $\hat{7}$. In the harmonic form of this scale, raised $\hat{7}$ is important when writing music and chords, but can sound strange when played by itself in the scale. When we raise and lower $\hat{6}$ and $\hat{7}$, the scale works better within a melody. Since this scale helps create smoother melodies, it is called the melodic minor scale.

Compare the A natural minor scale and the A melodic minor scale in Figure 8.13. In the melodic minor, $\hat{6}$ and $\hat{7}$ (F and G) are raised ascending and lowered descending. This scale contains both the leading tone (G♯) and the subtonic (G♮).

Figure 8.13

A natural minor

A melodic minor

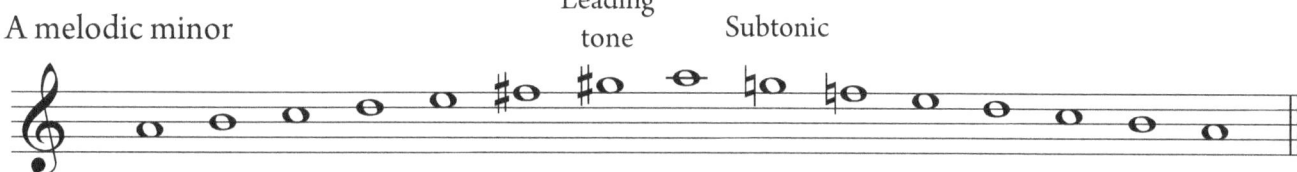

In a scale like G melodic minor you need to use a natural and a sharp to raise $\hat{6}$ and $\hat{7}$ ascending and a natural and flat to lower them descending (Figure 8.14).

Figure 8.14

1. The following are natural minor scales. Name the key of each. Add accidentals making them melodic minor scales. Mark the leading tone (LT) and subtonic (ST) in each.

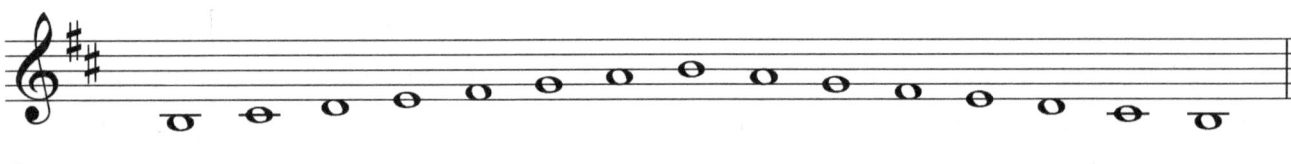

key:

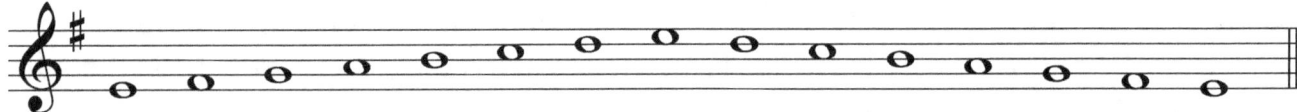

key:

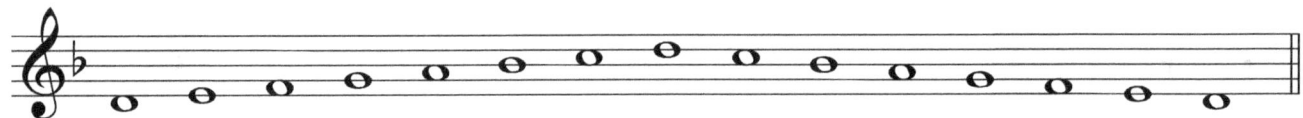

key:

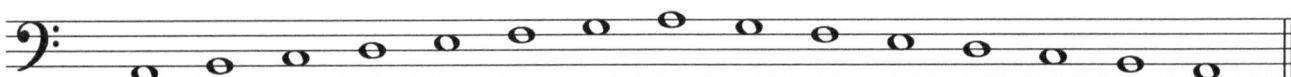

key:

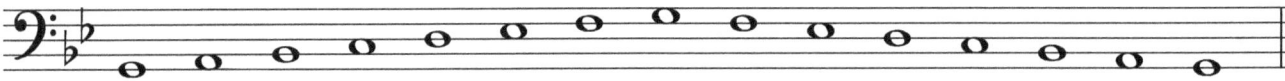

key:

❸ 2. Write the following scales ascending and descending in whole notes using a key signature.

G melodic minor

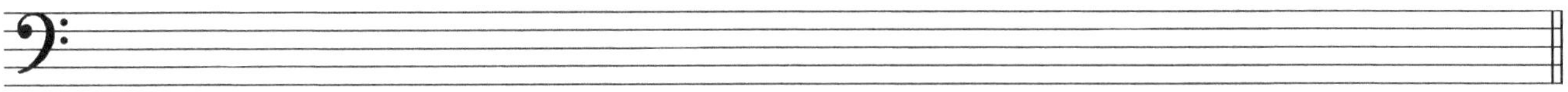

A melodic minor

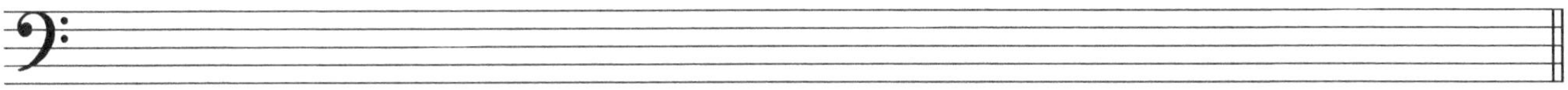

E melodic minor

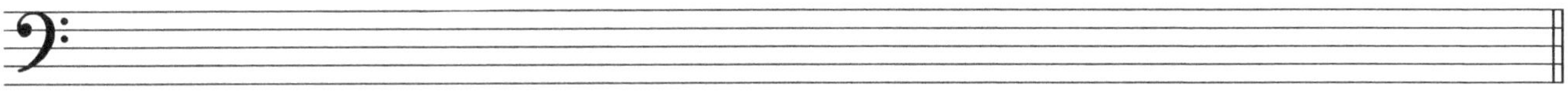

B melodic minor

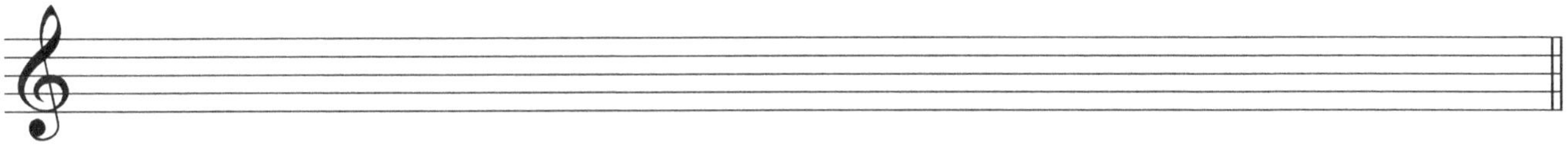

D melodic minor

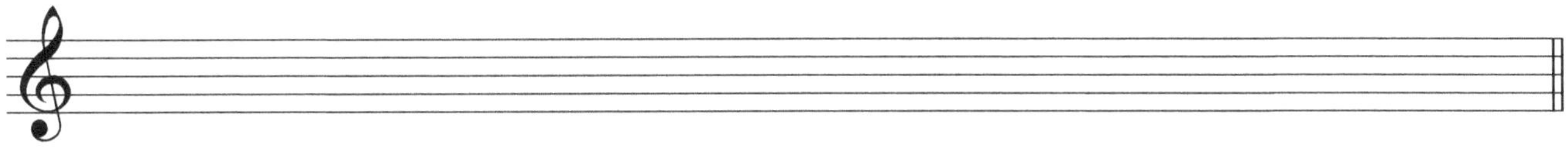

G melodic minor

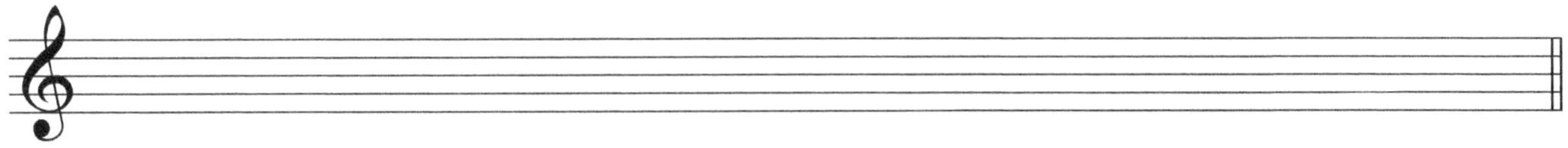

Minor Scales

❸3. Name the following minor scales.

Scale: _____

Scale: _____

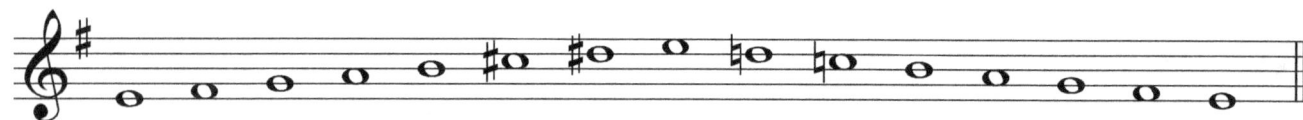

Scale: _____

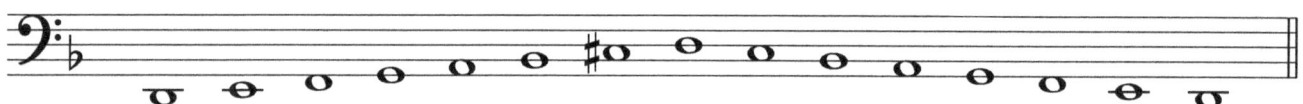

Scale: _____

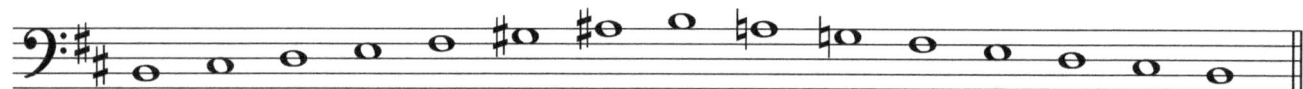

Scale: _____

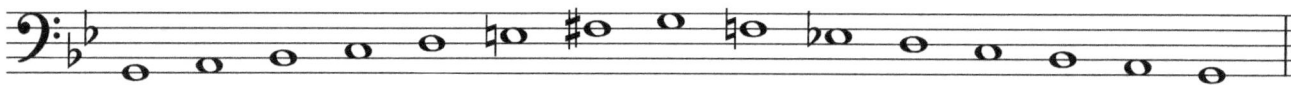

Scale: _____

❸ 4. Write the following scales ascending and descending in whole notes.

A melodic minor

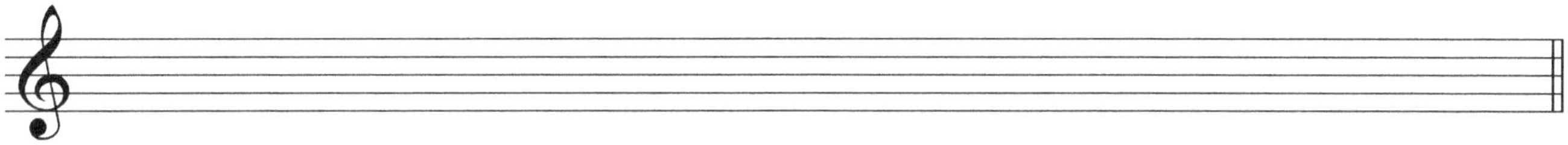

G harmonic minor

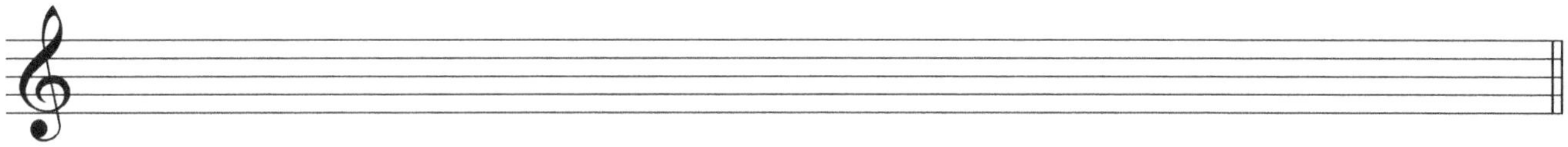

E melodic minor

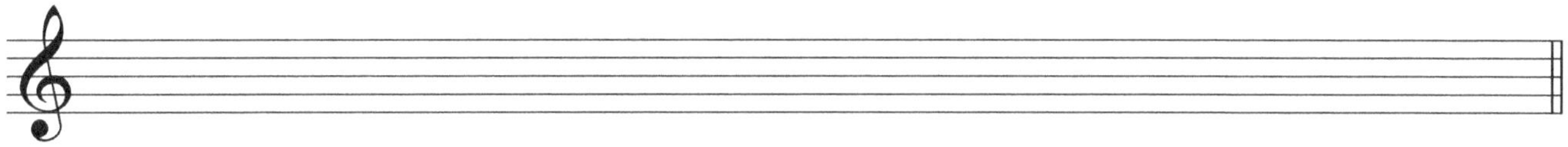

B harmonic minor

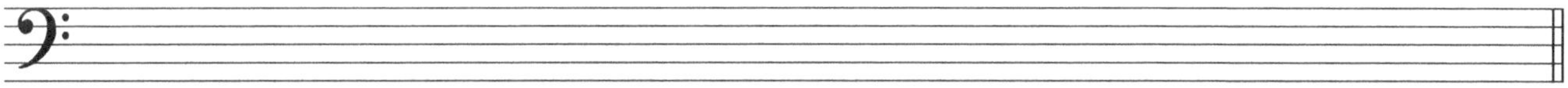

D natural minor

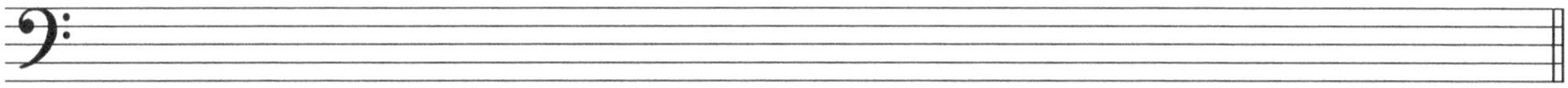

G melodic minor

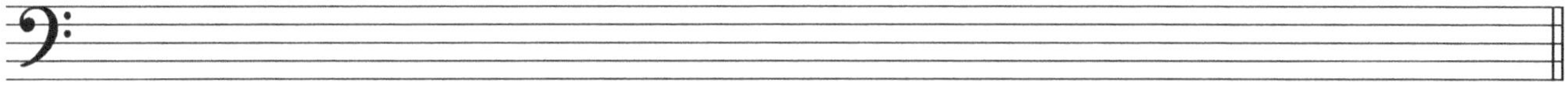

9
Intervals 2

❸Interval Review

An *interval* can be defined as the distance from one note to the next. An interval is indicated by a number. There are two basic types of intervals, **harmonic** and **melodic**.

- A harmonic interval occurs when two notes are played or sung at the same time.
- A melodic interval occurs when two notes are played or sung one after the other.

Figure 9.1

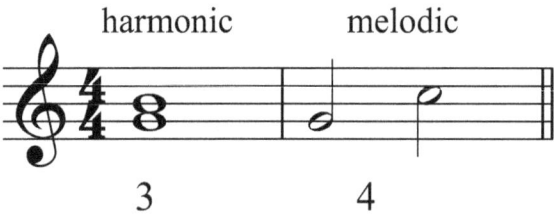

❸1. Write the number for the following intervals.

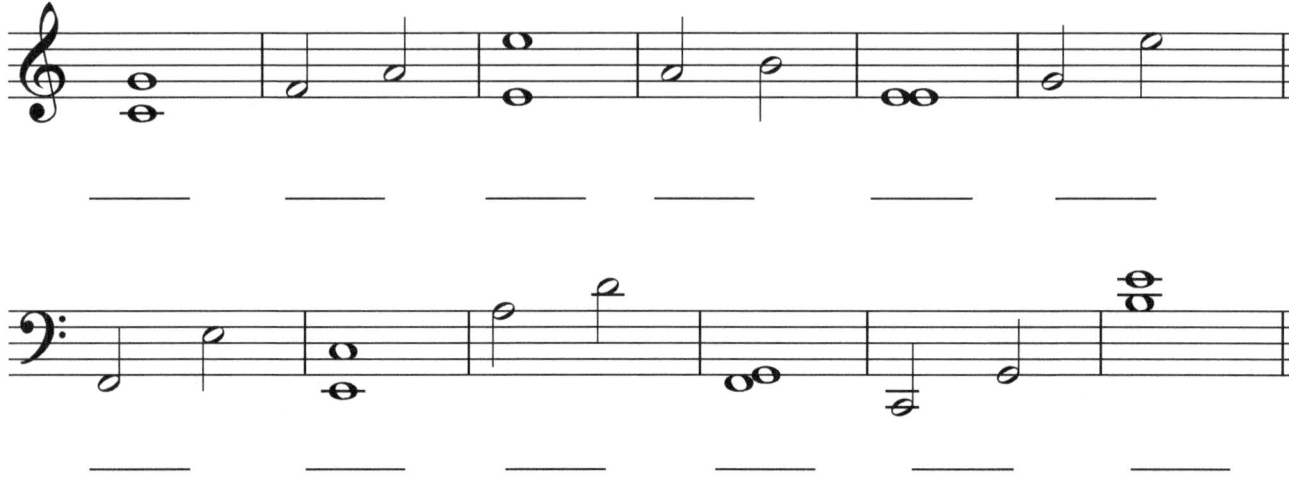

Intervals in Major and Minor Scales

Intervals can be built on the tonic of the major or minor scale. Figure 9.2 shows the intervals built on the tonic (G) of the G major scale. The interval of a 7th must be G-F♯ since the scale of G major has an F♯.

Figure 9.2

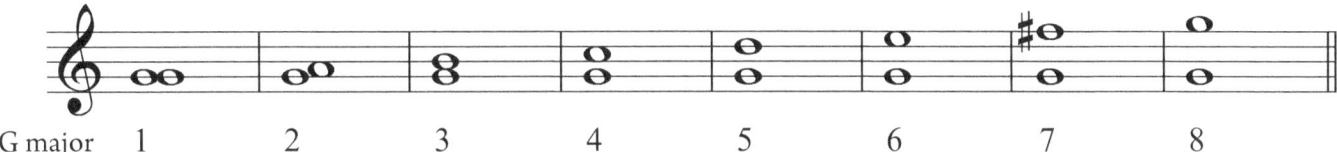

G major   1   2   3   4   5   6   7   8

If we write intervals on the tonic of the scale of D natural minor the 6th must contain a B♭ since B♭ is part of the D natural minor scale. Figure 9.3 shows the intervals built on the tonic of D natural minor.

Figure 9.3

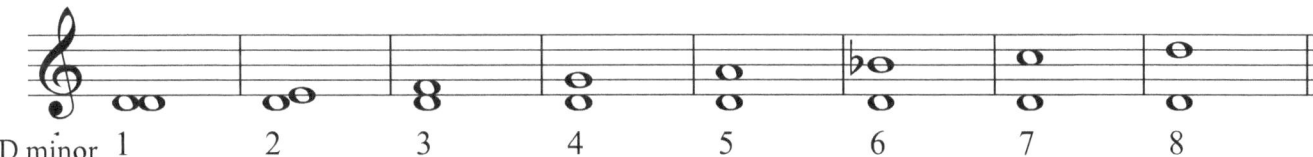

D minor   1   2   3   4   5   6   7   8

1. Write the following harmonic intervals on the tonic of the C major scale.

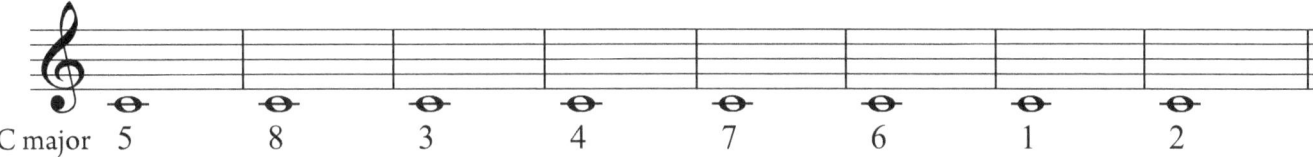

C major   5   8   3   4   7   6   1   2

2. Write the following harmonic intervals on the tonic of the F major scale. remember that F major has a B♭.

F major   8   4   5   3   2   1   6   7

3. Write the following melodic intervals on the tonic of the E natural minor scale. Remember that E minor has an F♯.

E minor   1   3   4   5   7   6   2   8

4. Write the following harmonic intervals on the tonic of the A natural minor scale.

A minor   2   3   1   6   4   5   8   7

5. Write the following melodic intervals on the tonic of the G major scale.

G major   8   1   4   6   7   5   2   3

❸ Interval Quality

As well as having a number, intervals also have a *quality*. We will begin our study with *major* and *perfect* intervals. Major and perfect are interval qualities. In order to understand how the qualities work we need to look at the major scale.

Major Intervals

The intervals that are major are: 2nds, 3rds, 6ths and 7ths. They are called major because of their sound. The symbol for a major interval is "maj" and looks like this:

maj 2   major second
maj 3   major third
maj 6   major sixth
maj 7   major seventh

In order for an interval to be major, the top note must be a member of the bottom notes scale. Figure 9.4 shows all the major intervals in D major. The major 3rd and the major 7th have sharps because in the scale of D major those two notes are sharp (F♯ and C♯). The top note of each interval belongs to the scale of D major. This is what makes them major intervals.

Figure 9.4

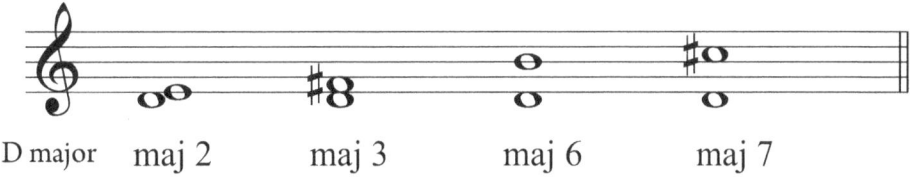

Perfect Intervals

The intervals that are perfect are: unisons (1s), 4ths, 5ths and octaves (8ths). They are called perfect because of their sound. The symbol for a perfect interval is "per" and looks like this:

per 1	perfect unison
per 4	perfect fourth
per 5	perfect fifth
per 8	perfect octave

In order for an interval to be perfect, like major, the top note must be a member of the bottom notes scale. Figure 9.5 shows all the perfect intervals in B♭ major. The top note of each interval belongs to the scale of B♭ major. This makes them perfect intervals.

Figure 9.5

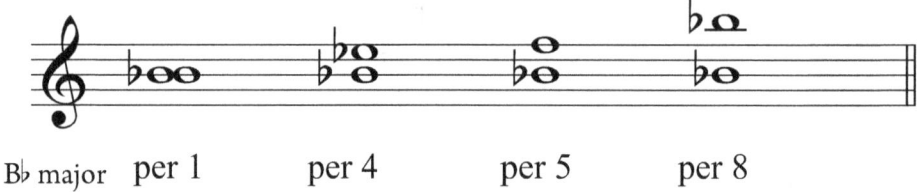

Figure 9.6 contains all the intervals in C major. The top note of each interval belongs to the C major scale. As a result of this, all of these intervals are major or perfect depending on their number.

Figure 9.6

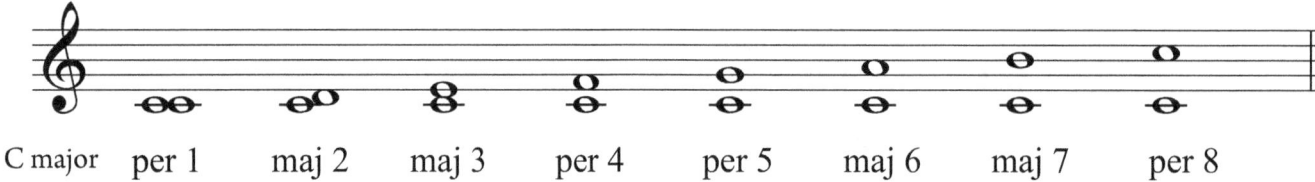

1. Write the following intervals in the key of G major. Use accidentals instead of a key signature.

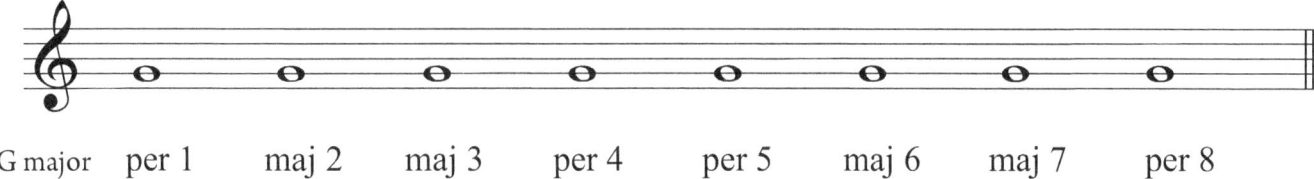

2. Write the following intervals in the key of F major. Use accidentals instead of a key signature.

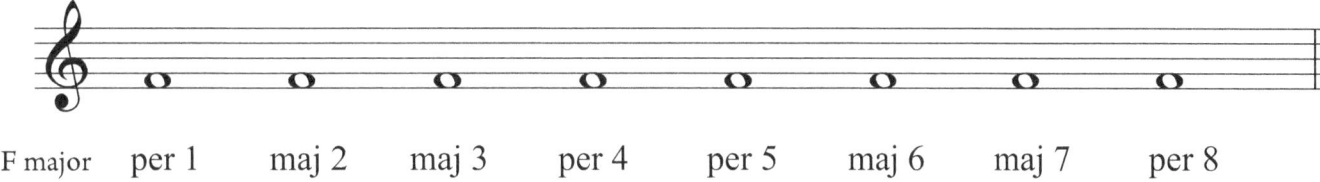

3. Name the following intervals. Think of the bottom note as the tonic of a major scale.

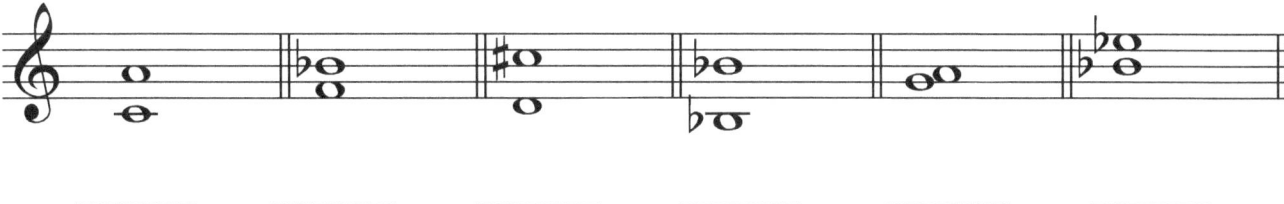

4. Write the following harmonic intervals above the given notes.

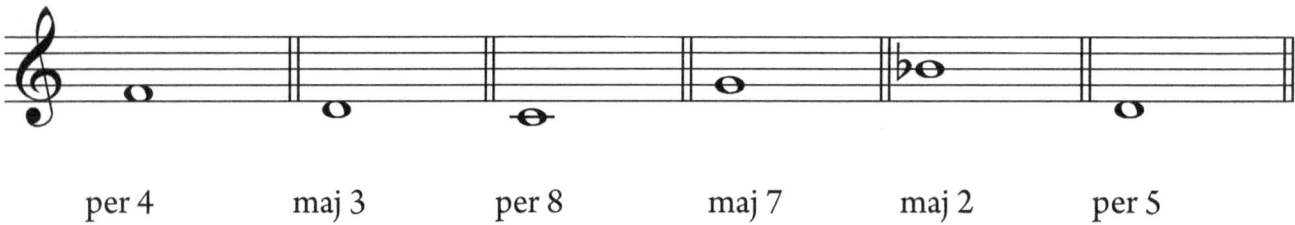

5. Write the following melodic intervals above the given notes.

❸ Minor Intervals

When we lower the upper note of a major interval by one half step, we get a ***minor interval***. Figure 9.7 contains a major 3rd and a minor 3rd in two keys. When we lower the upper note of the major 3rd by one half step we get a minor 3rd.

A major 3rd above C is E because E is the third note of the C major scale. If we lower the E to E♭, it is no longer part of the C scale and is a half step closer to C. This makes C to E♭ a minor 3rd.

A major 3rd above D is F♯ since the third note of the D major scale is F♯. In order to get a minor 3rd above D we lower the F♯ one half step to F♮.

Figure 9.7

❸1. Add an accidental lowering each major 3rd one half step to change it to a minor 3rd.

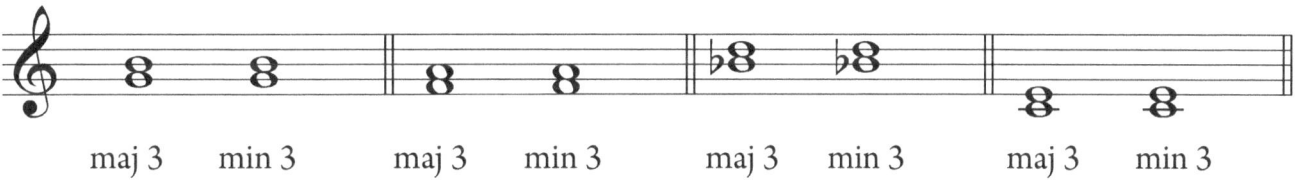

2. Name the following intervals as major 3rds or minor 3rds.

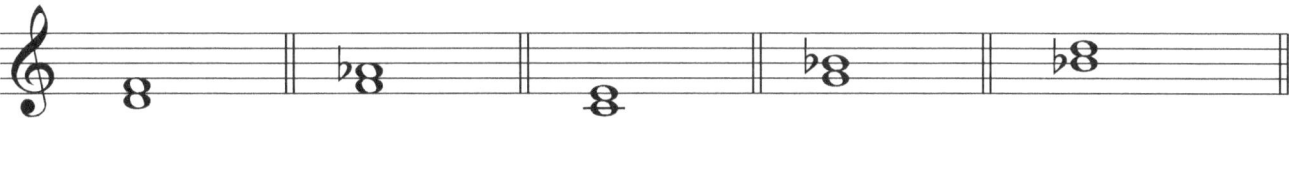

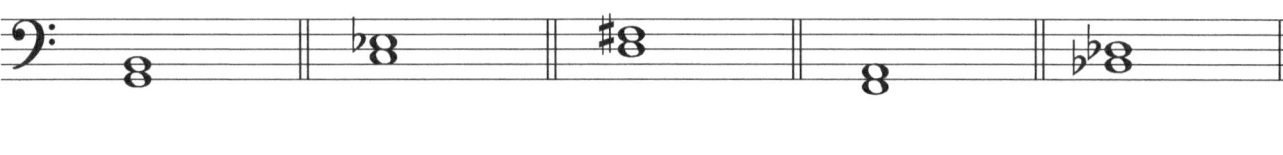

❸ 3. Write harmonic intervals above the following notes.

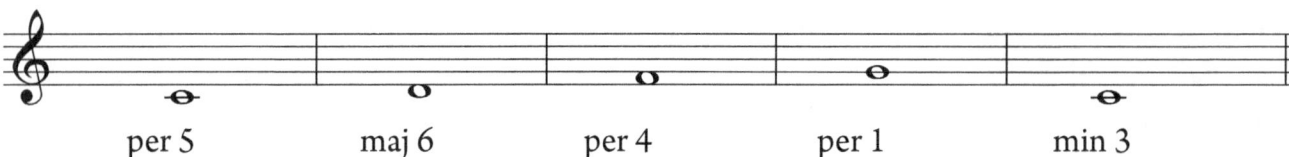

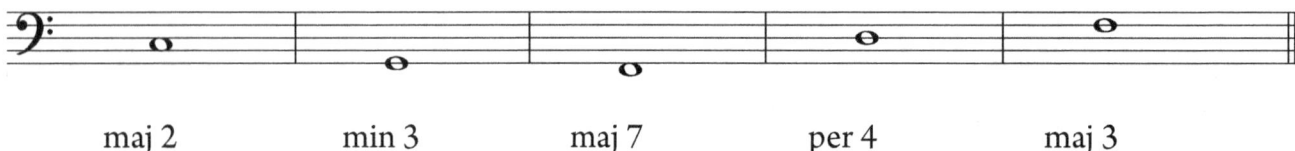

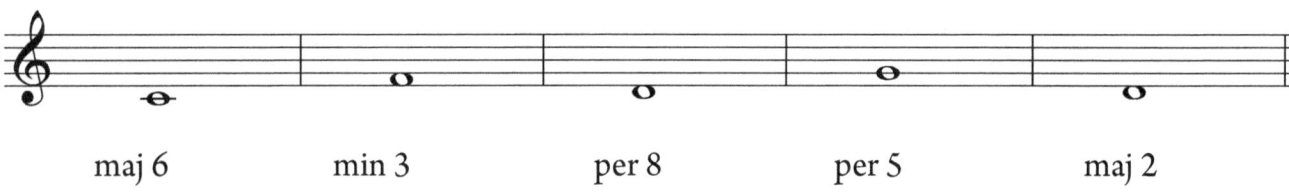

4. Name the following intervals.

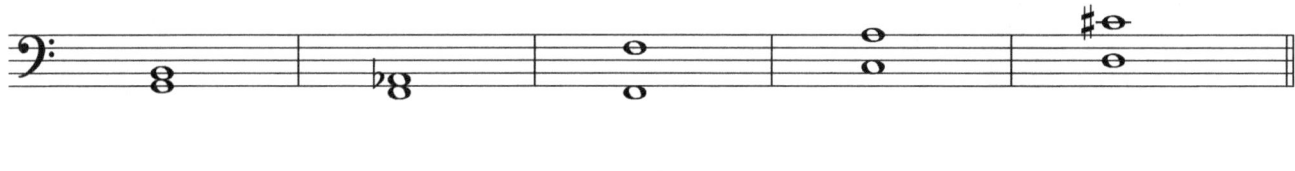

10

Chords

The Triad

A *chord* is three or more notes sounded at the same time. A *triad* is a three note chord. The *tonic triad* of any key is the triad built on $\hat{1}$ of the scale or the tonic. Figure 10.1 is the tonic triad in C major. The note that the triad is built on is called the *root*. The next note a third above it is called the *third*. The note a fifth above the root is called the *fifth*.

Figure 10.1

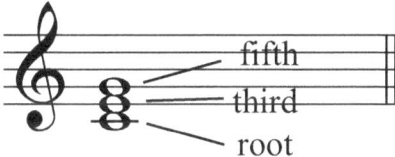

The tonic triad of C major is built on scale degrees $\hat{1}$, $\hat{3}$, and $\hat{5}$ of the C major scale (Figure 10.2). This is also called the ***C major triad***. You can build tonic triads in any key by stacking $\hat{1}$, $\hat{3}$, and $\hat{5}$ of the major scale on top of each other.

Figure 10.2

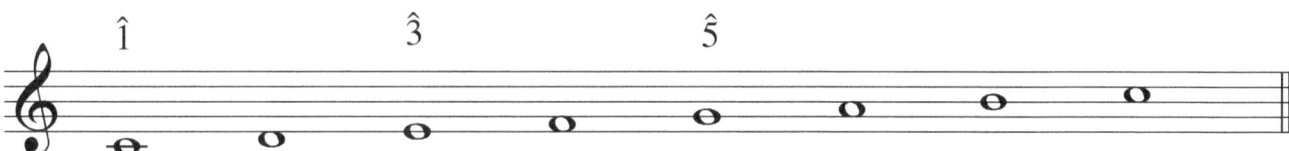

The tonic triad of G major is G-B-D. It is built like all tonic triads on $\hat{1}$, $\hat{3}$, and $\hat{5}$ of the major scale. The root is G. The 3rd is B, and the 5th is D. This is also called the G major triad.

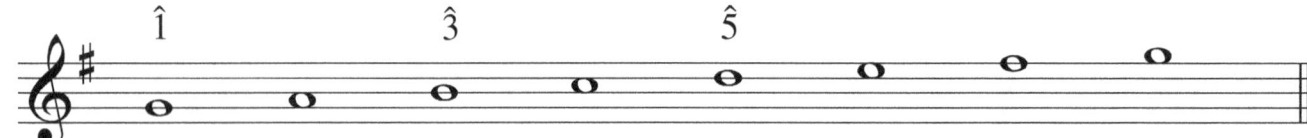

The tonic triad of F major is F-A-C. It is built like all tonic triads on $\hat{1}$, $\hat{3}$, and $\hat{5}$ of the major scale. The root is F. The 3rd is A and the 5th is C. This is also called the F major triad.

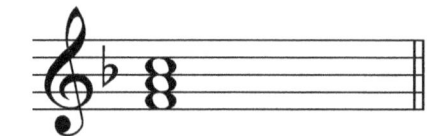

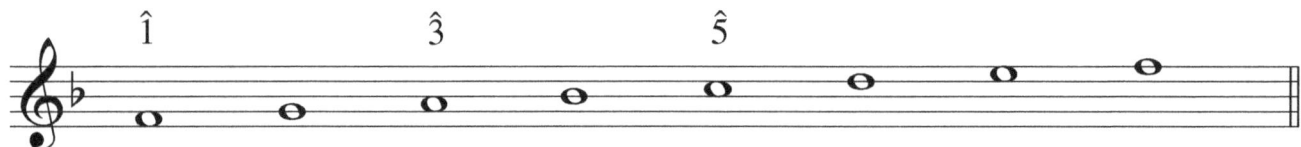

The tonic triad of A minor is A-C-E. It is built like all tonic triads on $\hat{1}$, $\hat{3}$, and $\hat{5}$, but this time we build it on the natural minor scale. The root is A. The 3rd is C and the 5th is E. This is also called the A minor triad.

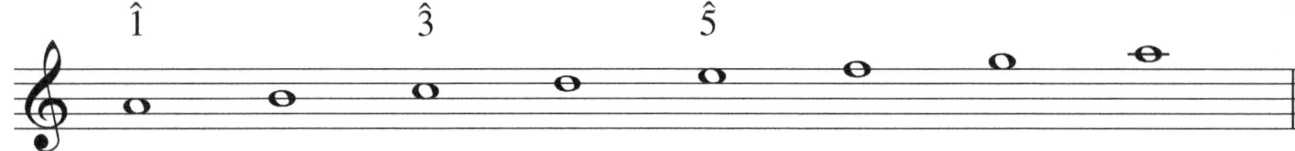

Chords

❶ 1. Write tonic triads in C, F, G major, and A minor using key signatures.
❷   Name the root, 3rd and 5th of each.
❸

Root: _____	Root: _____	Root: _____	Root: _____
Third: _____	Third: _____	Third: _____	Third: _____
Fifth: _____	Fifth: _____	Fifth: _____	Fifth: _____

❶
❷ Solid and Broken Triads
❸

A triad can be written and played **solid** or **broken**. A triad is solid when all the notes are played together or at the same time as in Figure 10.3. Another word for solid is **blocked**. A triad is broken when the notes are played one after the other as in Figure 10.4.

Figure 10.3   Figure 10.4

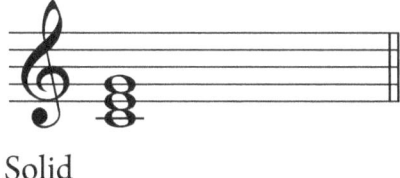   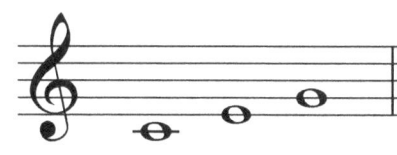

Solid   Broken

© San Marco Publications 2023   Chords

2. Name the following triads as C major, G major, etc.

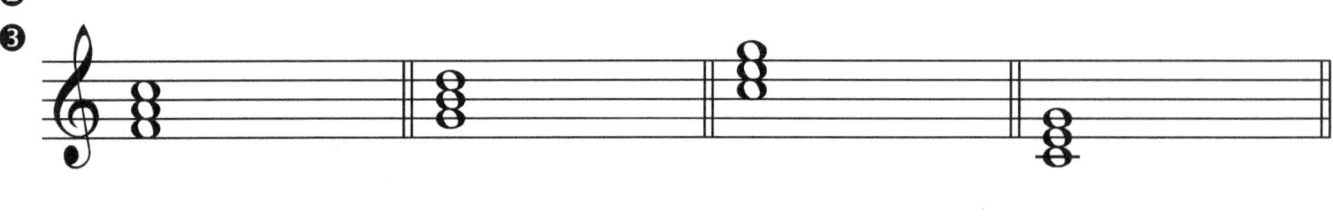

_____   _____   _____   _____

_____   _____   _____   _____

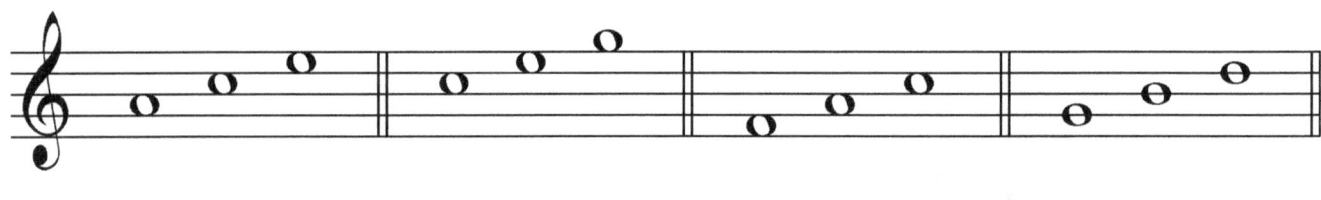

_____   _____   _____   _____

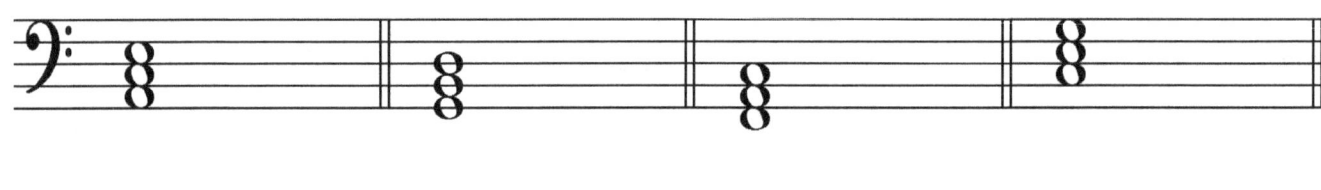

_____   _____   _____   _____

3. Write the following broken tonic triads in each clef. Use a key signature for each.

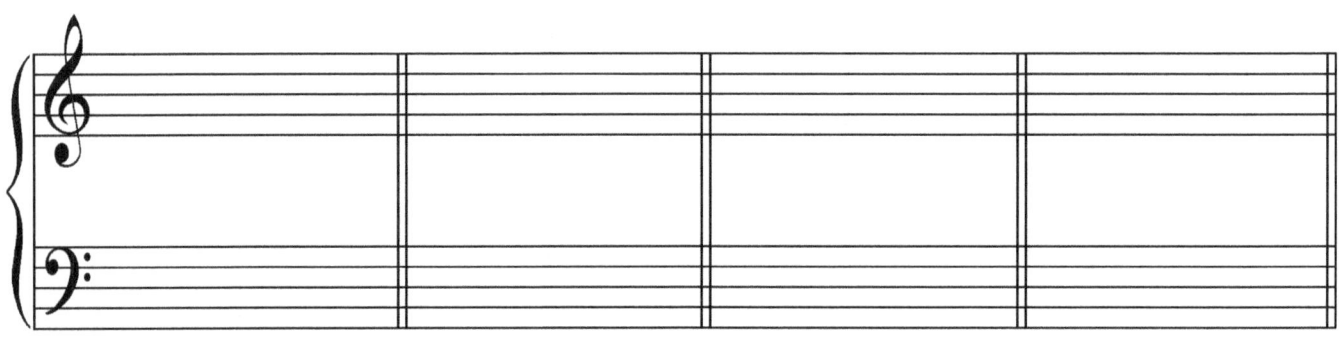

C major   F major   G major   A minor

❶ 4. Write the following solid tonic triads in each clef. Use a key signature for each.
❷
❸

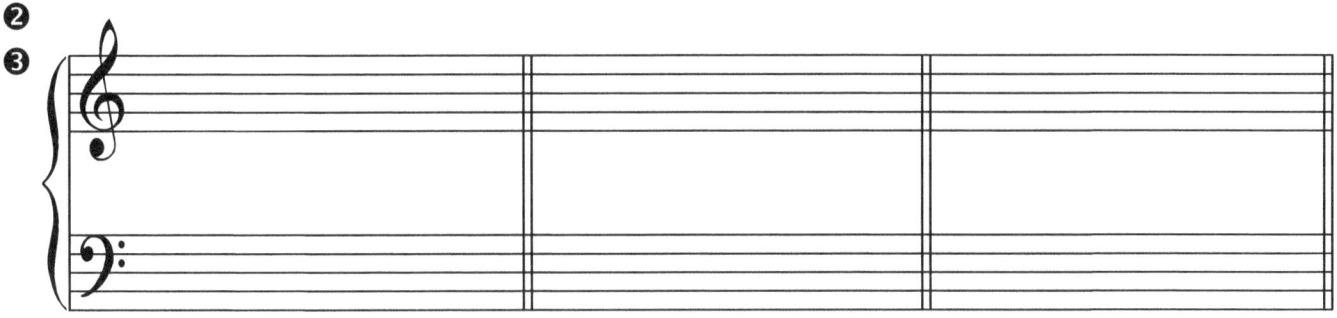

            G major   A minor   F major

5. Name the root, 3rd, and 5th of the following triads.

Triad	Root	3rd	5th
F major	_____	_____	_____
G major	_____	_____	_____
C major	_____	_____	_____
A minor	_____	_____	_____

6. Name the key for each of the following. Circle three notes that can form the tonic triad.

Chords

Tonic Triads in Major and Minor Keys

A triad can be built on the tonic of a major scale by stacking thirds on the first note. This results in a ***major triad***. A triad built on the tonic of any major scale is a major triad. Figure 10.5 shows the G major triad, which is built on the tonic of the G major scale. We classify triads with figures called ***chord symbols***. There are two types shown here. One is the ***root/quality chord symbol*** which occurs above the triad. Since this is a G major triad the root/quality symbol is an upper case G. The other symbol occurs below the triad and is the upper case Roman numeral I. This indicates that this is the triad built on scale degree 1̂ of the key. We are in the key of G major here and the triad is built on G. This is called a ***functional chord symbol***.

Figure 10.5

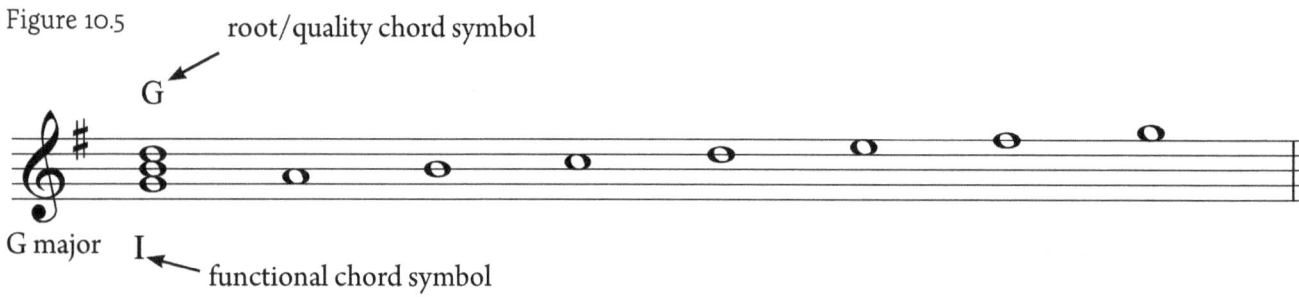

A triad built on the tonic of a minor scale results is a ***minor triad***. Any triad built on the tonic of a minor scale is a minor triad. Figure 10.6 shows the E minor triad built on the tonic of the E natural minor scale. The root/quality chord symbol for a minor triad is the letter name plus the letter m. In this case **Em**. Some books will use the symbol Emin. The functional chord symbol is a lowercase Roman numeral **i**. This indicates that it is built on scale degree 1̂ of E minor. The lowercase 'i' means that the chord is minor.

Figure 10.6

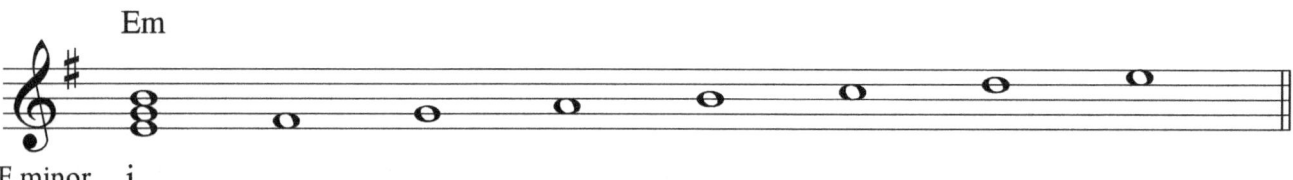

❷ Figure 10.7 shows solid (blocked) triads built on the tonic notes of three major keys with their key
❸ signatures and chord symbols.

Figure 10.7

Figure 10.8 shows broken triads built on the tonics of three major keys with their key signatures and chord symbols. Broken triads may ascend or descend.

Figure 10.8

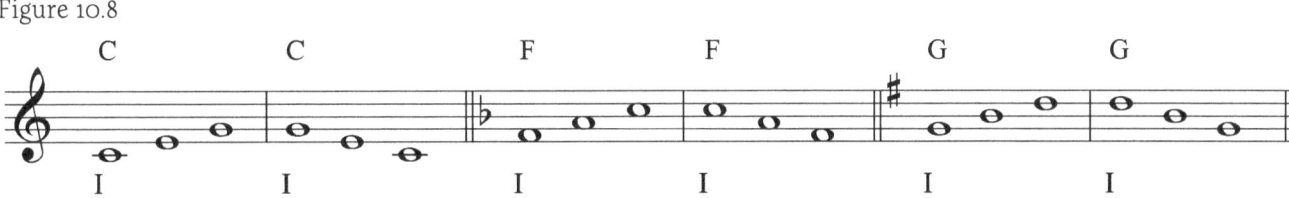

Figure 10.9 shows solid triads built on the tonics of three minor keys with their key signatures and chord symbols.

Figure 10.9

Figure 10.10 shows broken triads built on the tonics of three minor keys with their key signatures and chord symbols.

Figure 10.10

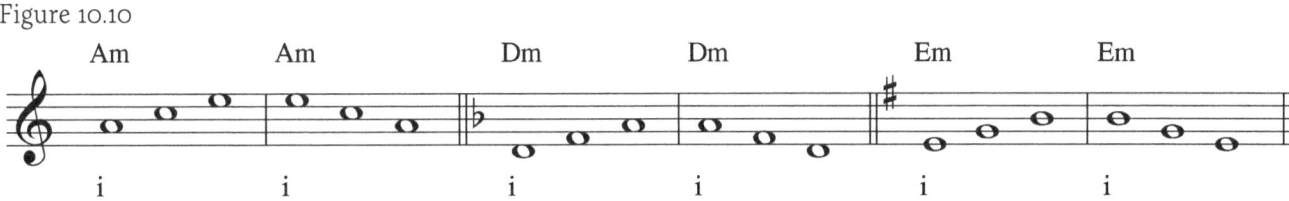

1. The following are all tonic triads. Name the key. Write the root/quality and functional chord symbol for each.

2. Write tonic triads in the following keys in solid form. Use a key signature for each. Add the root/quality and functional chord symbols.

    A minor   G major   D minor   C major   F major   E minor

    E minor   C major   A minor   F major   D minor   G major

❷ 3. Write the following tonic triads in broken form according to the root/quality and functional
❸   chord symbols. Use key signatures for each.

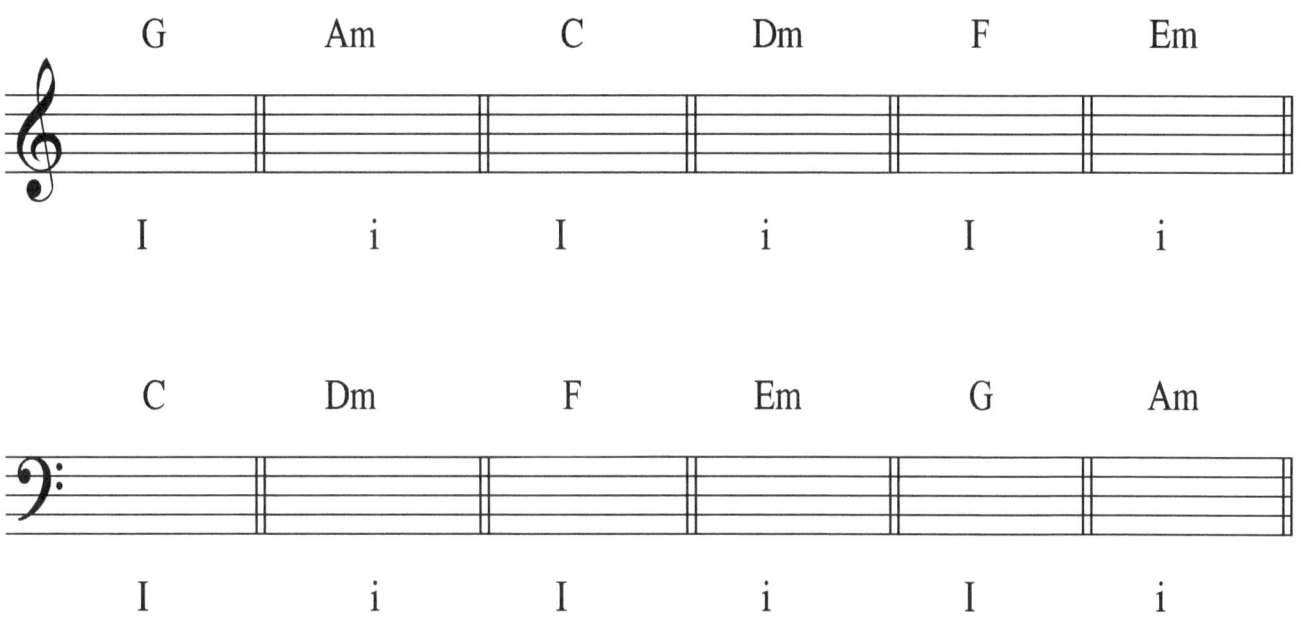

4. For the following descending broken triads: Name the key. Write the root/quality chord
   symbol. Name the root, 3rd and 5th of each.

key: _____	key: _____	key: _____
root: _____	root: _____	root: _____
3rd: _____	3rd: _____	3rd: _____
5th: _____	5th: _____	5th: _____

key: _____	key: _____	key: _____
root: _____	root: _____	root: _____
3rd: _____	3rd: _____	3rd: _____
5th: _____	5th: _____	5th: _____

Music Terms

Study the following music terms.

poco	little
molto	much, very
fine	the end
da capo, D.C.	from the beginning
D.C. al fine	repeat from the beginning and end at *fine*.

Triads in Major Keys

A triad can be built on any note of the major scale just by stacking two thirds on top of the note. In this level, we will cover triads built on $\hat{1}$ and $\hat{5}$. Scale degree $\hat{1}$ is the tonic. A triad built on the tonic of a major scale is called the **tonic triad**. Scale degree $\hat{5}$ is the dominant. A triad built on the dominant of a major scale is called the **dominant triad**. Figure 10.11 contains triads built on $\hat{1}$ and $\hat{5}$ of the C major scale. The root of the triad built on $\hat{1}$ in C major is C. The root of the triad built on $\hat{5}$ in C major is G. The root/quality chord symbols **C** and **G** are placed above the staff. The Roman numerals, called the functional chord symbols **I** and **V** are placed below the staff.

Figure 10.11

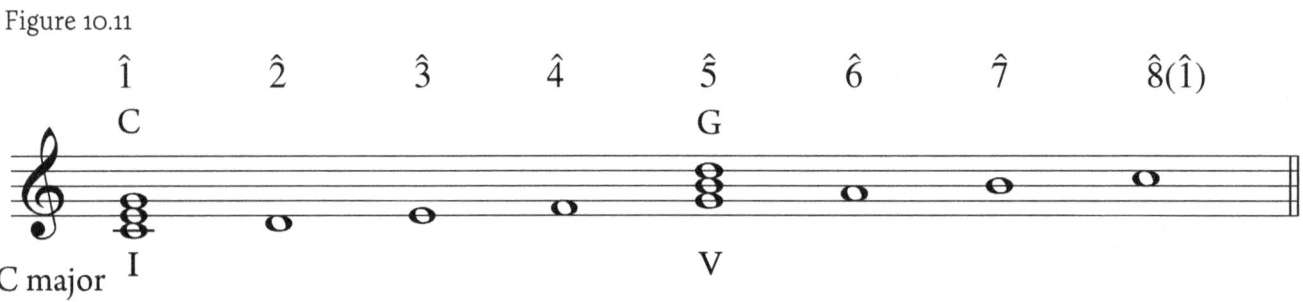

❸ 1. Name the key of the folowing scales and write triads on the tonic and dominant notes. Add Roman numeral and root/quality chord symbols for each.

key:

key:

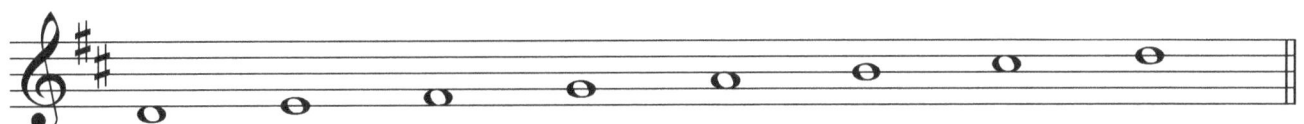

key:

key:

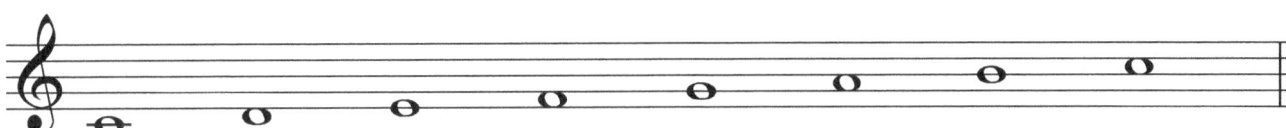

key:

❸ 2. Write the following triads using accidentals instead of a key signature. Add the functional and root/quality chords symbols for each.

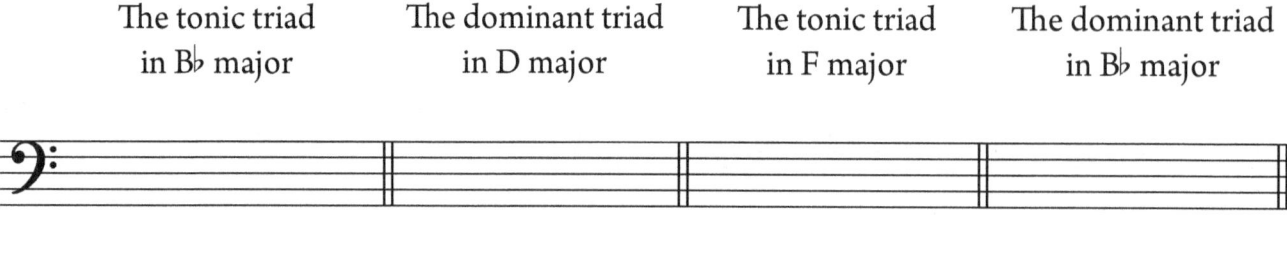

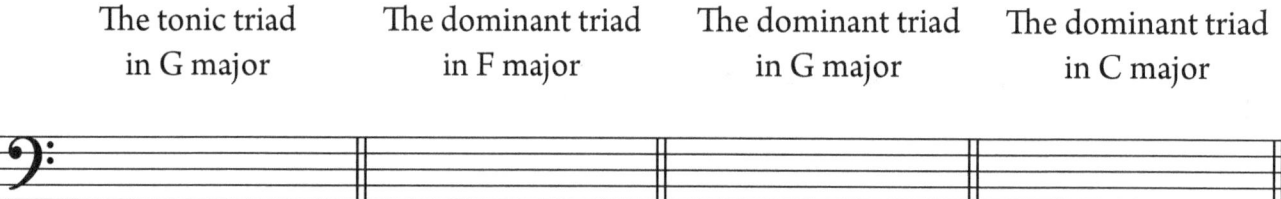

❸ Triads in Minor Keys

Triads are also found in minor keys. Just like in major keys, we can build a triad on $\hat{1}$ or $\hat{5}$ of the harmonic minor scale to get the tonic and dominant triads in a minor key. It is important to note that the dominant triad in a minor key has raised $\hat{7}$ to reflect the harmonic form of the scale. Dominant triads in minor keys will always have an accidental for now. The third of the dominant triad is raised one half step because it is the leading tone. Figure 10.12 contains the tonic and dominant triads in A minor. The Roman numeral symbols for these chords are a lowercase "**i**" for the tonic triad and an uppercase "**V**" for the dominant triad. Raised $\hat{7}$ in A minor is G♯ and it is the third of the dominant triad. The root/quality symbol for the A minor triad is **Am**.

Figure 10.12

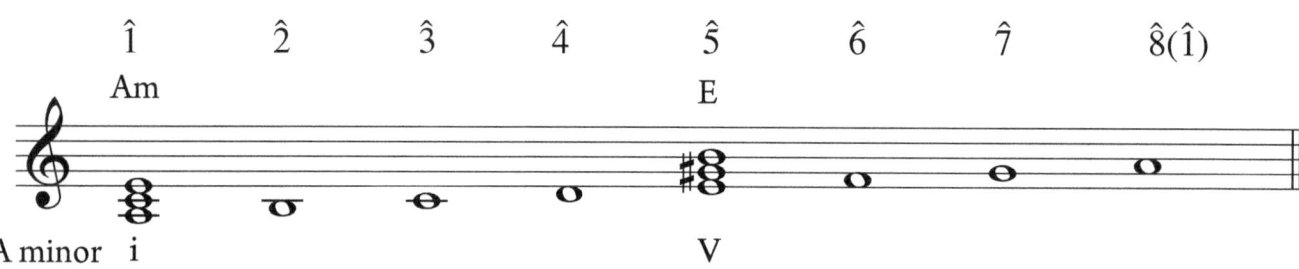

1. Name the key of the following harmonic minor scales. Write triads on the tonic and dominant notes. Add the Roman numeral and root/quality chord symbols for each.

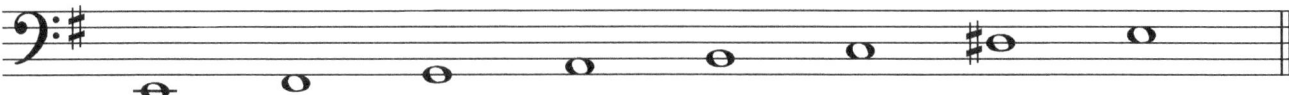

key:

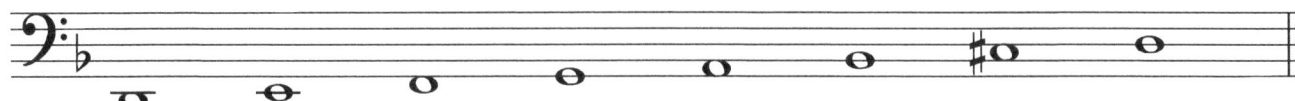

key:

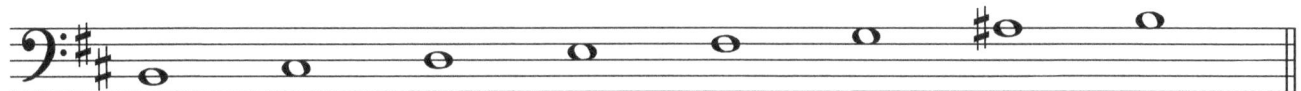

key:

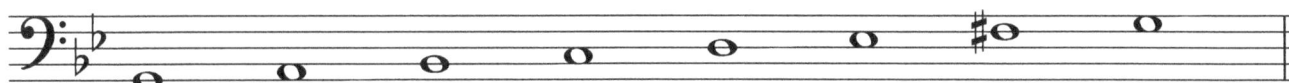

key:

key:

❸ 2. Write the following triads using accidentals instead of a key signature. Add the Roman numeral and root/quality chords symbols for each.

| The tonic triad in A minor | The dominant triad in B minor | The tonic triad in E minor | The dominant triad in G minor |

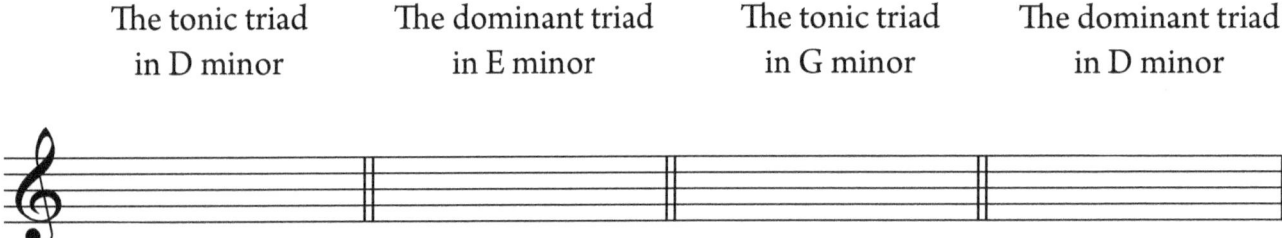

| The tonic triad in D minor | The dominant triad in E minor | The tonic triad in G minor | The dominant triad in D minor |

3. Name the minor key for the following. Add the chord symbol under each and label them as tonic or dominant triads.

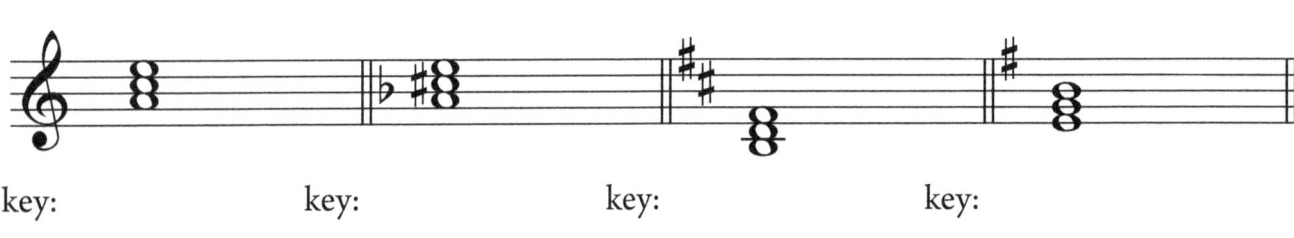

key: key: key: key:

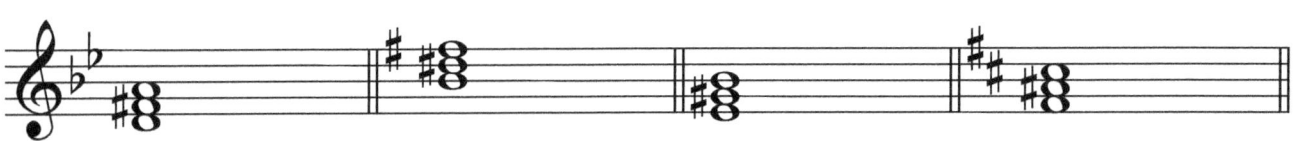

key: key: key: key:

11
Melody

What is melody?

Most musical compositions have a line of notes that are played one after the other to form a tune. This is called a *melody*. A melody is the main tune of a song. Figure 11.1 is the popular melody 'Mary had a Little Lamb.'

Figure 11.1

The Phrase

Most traditional melodies move in four measure sections called *phrases*. A phrase is like a musical sentence. Like the sentence in a story, a phrase represents one musical idea. A phrase is indicated by a long curved line called a *phrase mark*. A phrase mark looks like a large slur. This line indicates the beginning and end of the phrase. Figure 11.1 contains a phrase mark above the melody. This melody is four measures long, which is the most common length of a musical phrase.

How a Melody Moves

The notes of a melody can move in different ways:

- They can move by **step**.
- They can move by **leap**.
- They can move **repetition**.

Most good melodies use all three types of movement. Figure 11.2 shows the three types of movement working together in the first two phrases of the melody 'Twinkle Twinkle Little Star.' Each phrase is four measures long. A leap is the interval of a 3rd or more. Here, the melody leaps a 5th from the last note of m.1 to the first note of m.2. (m. is an abbreviation for the word measure.)

Figure 11.2

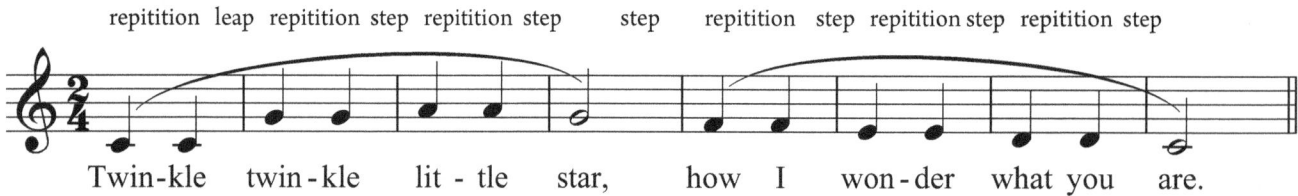

1. Name the key and mark the steps (S), leaps (L), and repetition (R) in the following melodies.

English Folk Song

key:

Norwegian Folk Song

key:

Writing a Stepwise Melody

In this lesson, we are going to learn to write melodies that move by step. The melody in Figure 11.3 moves by step. It is in G major and uses the notes of the G major scale. It is four measures long and begins and ends on the tonic (G). The tonic is like home base for a piece of music. You can expect to see the tonic used frequently. A piece in the key of G major is all about G. Often a piece in G will start and end on G and contain many G's throughout. G, the tonic, is the star of a piece in G major. This melody has a natural arch that peaks at E. E is the **climax** or high point of the melody. Many melodies will have one high note that is the climax and not repeated. The rhythm of the melody is indicated above the staff.

Figure 11.3

G major

The melody in Figure 11.4 moves entirely by step. It is in F major and uses the notes of the F major scale. There is a compositonal device called a **motive** in this melody. A motive is a melodic and rhythmic idea repeated higher or lower. The motive in m.1 is repeated a step higher in m.2 before the melody steps down to the tonic. This melody begins and ends on the tonic (F). It is the strongest way to begin and end a melody because the tonic is the most prominent note in any key. It clearly establishes F major as the key.

Figure 11.4

F major

Melody

❶ 1. Complete this melody using the notes of the C major scale and the given rhythm. Use stepwise
❷ motion or repeated notes, ending on the tonic (1̂). Draw a line marking the phrase.
❸

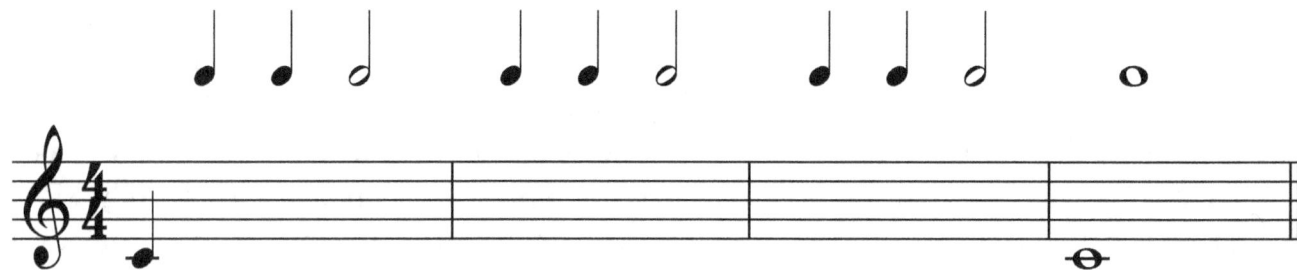

2. Complete this melody using the notes of the F major scale and the given rhythm. Use stepwise motion or repeated notes, ending on the tonic (1̂). Draw a line marking the phrase.

3. Complete this melody using the notes of the G major scale and the given rhythm. Use stepwise motion or repeated notes, ending on the tonic (1̂). Draw a line marking the phrase.

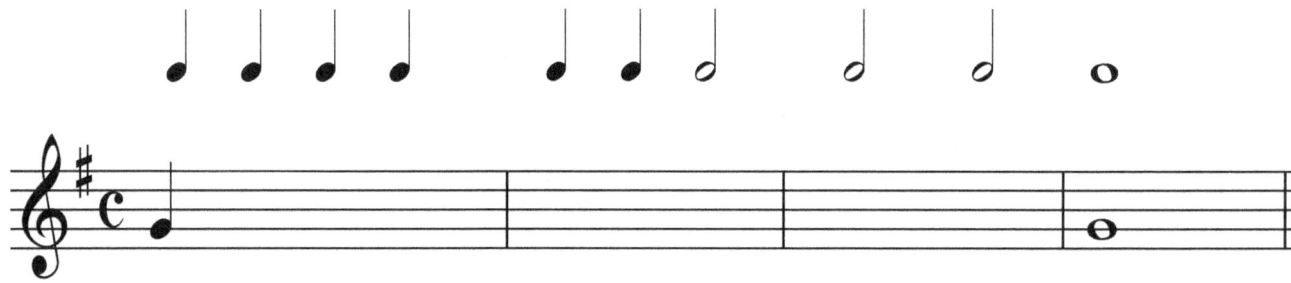

Stable Pitches

The strongest and most ***stable pitch*** of any key is the tonic. A stable pitch is a note that has strength, finality, and completeness. Many melodies begin and end on the tonic. The melody in Figure 11.5 is in the key of G major and begins and ends on the tonic ($\hat{1}$).

Figure 11.5

G major

Another relatively stable pitch, is scale degree $\hat{3}$. Scale degree $\hat{3}$, is the 3rd of the tonic triad and has a certain amount of strength and stability, although it is not as strong as $\hat{1}$. The melody in Figure 11.6 ends on $\hat{3}$.

Figure 11.6

G major

Unstable Pitches

Some pitches within a key are considered ***unstable***. An unstable pitch is a note that lacks finality or completeness. A composition would not end on an unstable pitch, but a phrase might. One unstable pitch is scale degree $\hat{2}$. If scale degree $\hat{1}$ is like a period at the end of a sentence, scale degree $\hat{2}$ is like a question mark. It needs an answer to complete it. The melody in Figure 11.7 ends on scale degree $\hat{2}$.

Figure 11.7

G:

❷ 1. Name the major key of each melody. Write the scale degree number for the last note and mark
❸ it as stable or unstable.

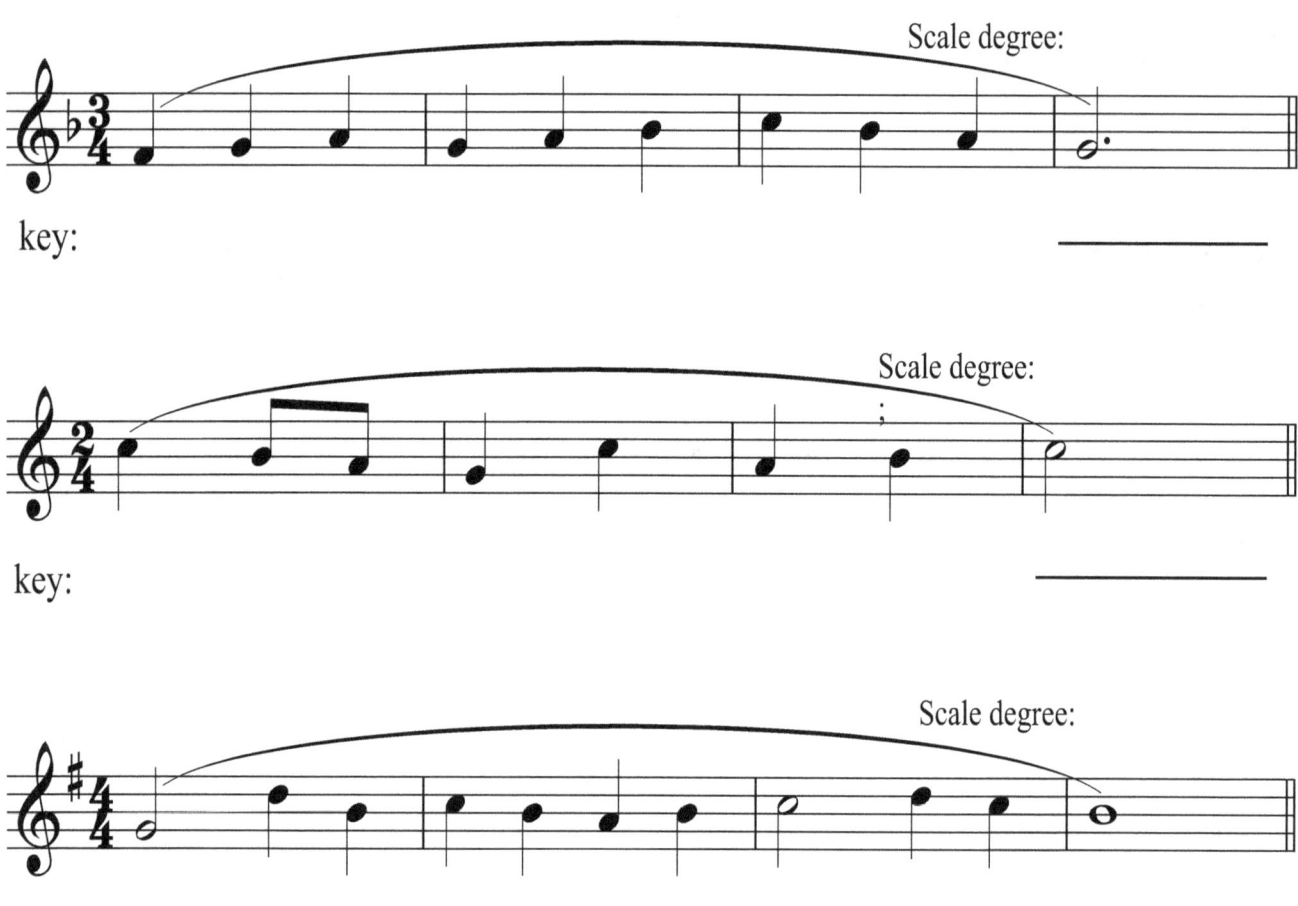

key:

key:

key:

The Motive

Many phrases are built from smaller groups of notes called ***motives***. A motive is a specific pattern of notes and rhythms. Motives can be repeated at a higher or lower pitch. Figure 11.8 contains a melodic motive in measure one consisting of a half note, two eighths and a quarter. The notes skip up a 3rd and then step down. In the two measures that follow, the motive is repeated a step higher each time.

Figure 11.8

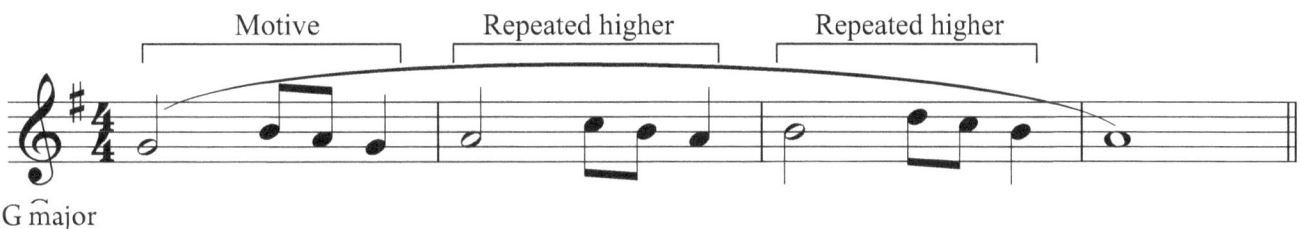

G major

1. Name the major key for each of the following melodies. Mark the phrases with slurs. Circle the melodic motives each time they occur in the melodies.

key:

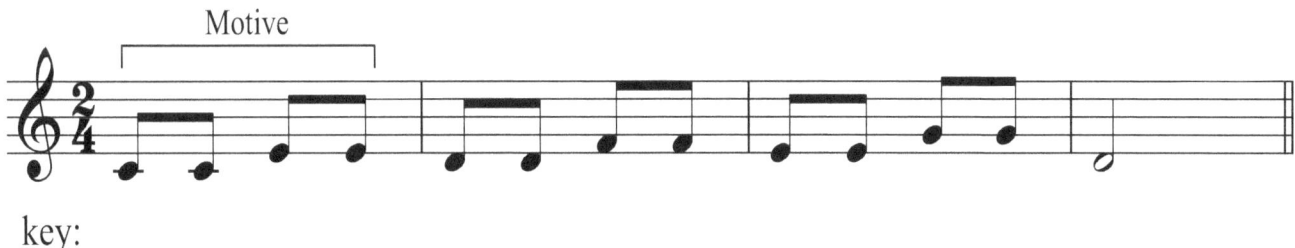

key:

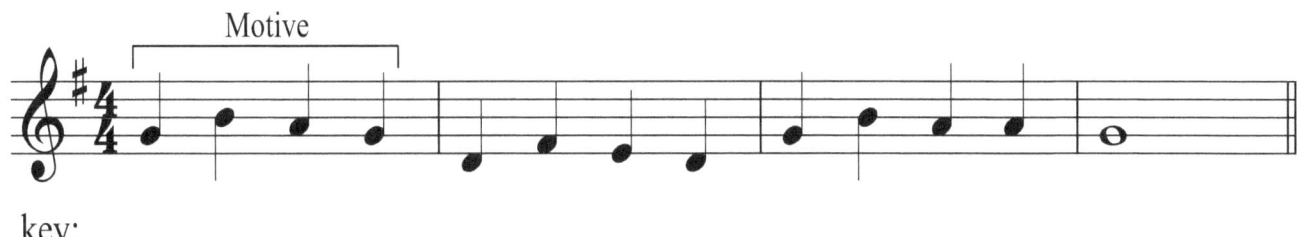

key:

²⁄₃ Writing Melodies

In this lesson we are going to learn to write melodies that use stepwise motion and skips of a 3rd using notes of the tonic triad. Figure 11.9 is a melody in C major. The first measure contains skips of 3rds outlining the tonic triad. The rest of the melody moves in stepwise motion. The first and the final note is $\hat{1}$, which is a stable scale degree in C major.

Figure 11.9

C major

Figure 11.10 is a melody in G major. This melody uses notes of the tonic triad in G and stepwise motion. It begins on scale degree $\hat{1}$ and ends on scale degree $\hat{3}$. Both of these are considerered stable scale degrees, since they are the first and third of the tonic triad. $\hat{3}$ is less strong sounding than $\hat{1}$. Scale degree $\hat{1}$ is the best choice for a final phrase of a piece where you want a strong, final ending. Beginning and ending on the tonic helps to confirm the key.

Figure 11.10

G major

1. Complete the following melody in C major, using the given rhythm. Use stepwise motion and skips. End on a stable pitch ($\hat{1}$ or $\hat{3}$).

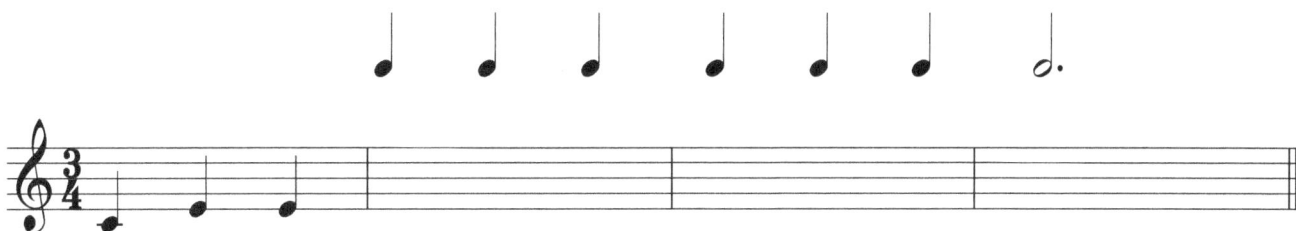

2. Complete the following melody in G major, using the given rhythm. Use stepwise motion and skips. End on a stable pitch ($\hat{1}$ or $\hat{3}$).

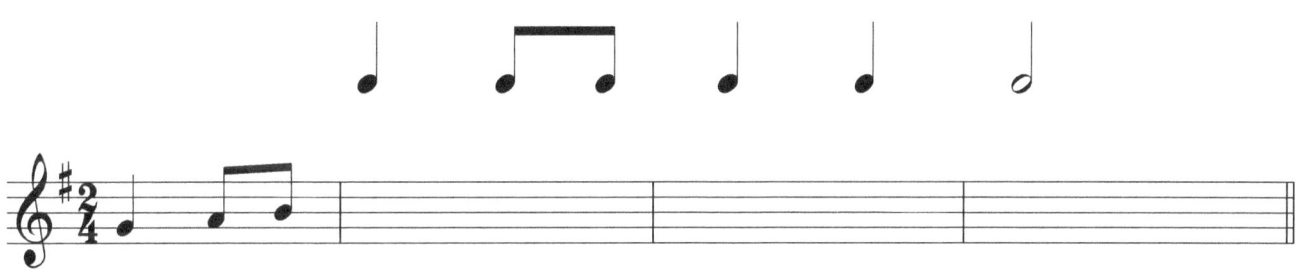

3. Complete the following melody in F major, using the given rhythm. Use stepwise motion and skips. End on a stable pitch ($\hat{1}$ or $\hat{3}$).

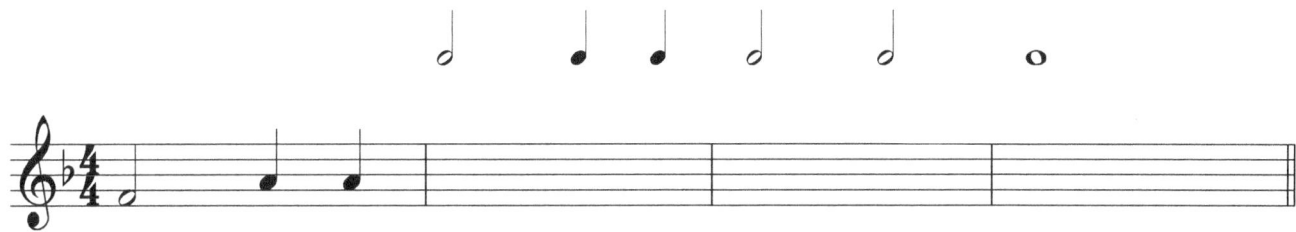

❷4. Compose a melody in F major, using the given rhythm. Use stepwise motion and skips. End on
❸   a stable pitch (1̂ or 3̂).

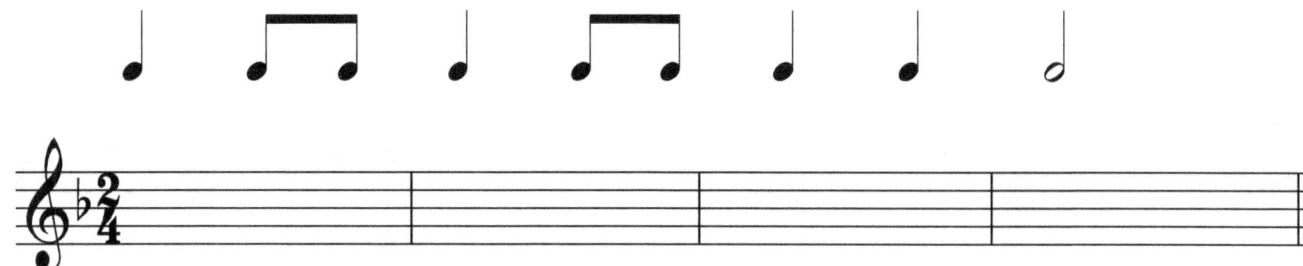

5. Compose a melody in G major, using the given rhythm. Use stepwise motion and skips. End on a stable pitch (1̂ or 3̂).

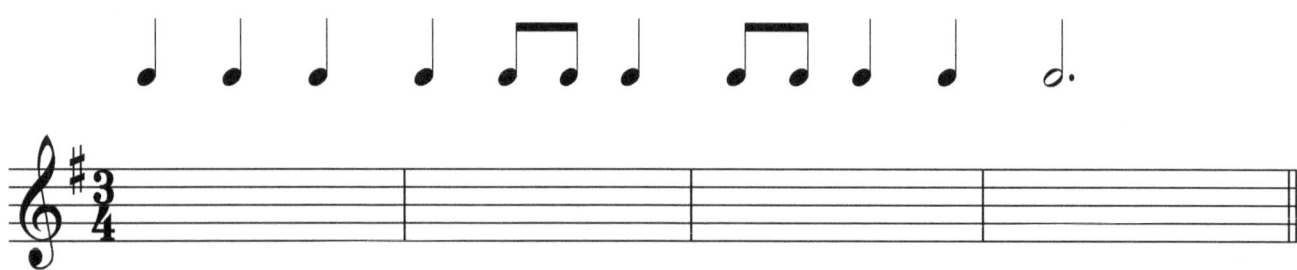

6. Compose a melody in C major, using the given rhythm. Use stepwise motion and skips. End on a stable pitch (1̂ or 3̂).

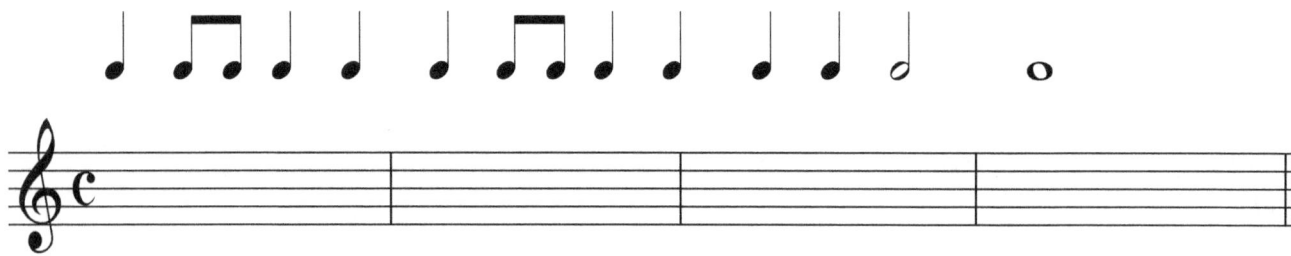

❸ Conjunct and Disjunct Motion

Melodies move in various ways. When a melody moves by step, the motion is called *conjunct motion*. When a melody moves by skip or leap, the motion is called **disjunct motion**. Good melodies are a combination of both of these. Let's compare a few melodies. The melody in Figure 11.11 consists only of disjunct motion. Every note leaps and there is no stepwise motion until the last two notes. The result is a fractured melody that would be very hard to sing and to play on some instruments.

Figure 11.11

G major

The melody in Figure 11.12 contains only conjunct or stepwise motion. Although it is not a terrible melody, using only scalewise motion is not very interesting.

Figure 11.12

G major

Figure 11.13 contains a melody that is a combination of conjunct and disjunct motion. The balance of both types of motion produces an interesting melody. It should be noted that this melody is in G major and both the tonic and dominant chords are outlined within it. The tonic chord (G B D) occurs in measure one and the dominant chord (D F♯ A) can be found in measure three. These are the two most prominent chords in any key. Using these chords creates a strong melody that is clearly based on the key of G major. In this level, we are going to write melodies that use stepwise motion and skips or leaps based on the tonic and dominant triads.

Figure 11.13

G major

Writing a Melody

The tonic and dominant chords are very strong elements to use in a melody. Figure 11.14 shows some of the ways the tonic triad in C major can be incorporated into a melody to add interest and variety with disjunct motion. Study the C major tonic triads used melodically.

    a) The tonic triad (C E G) is written into the melody creating skips of a 3rd.
    b) The skips are softened slightly with stepwise motion beween the 3rd and 5th (E F G).
    c) The stepwise motion may be placed between the root and 3rd (C D E).
    d) The triad may be outlined backwards from the 5th down to the root (G E C).

Figure 11.14

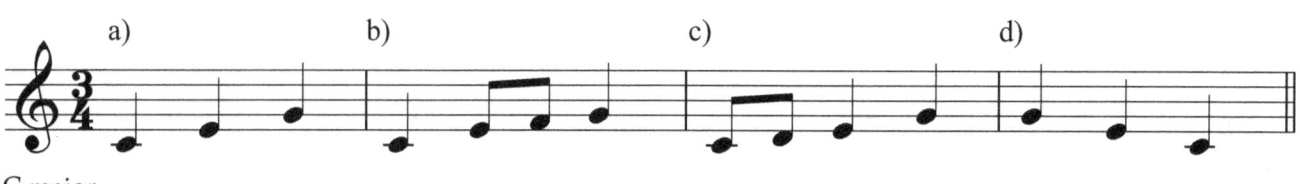

C major

The dominant triad is also effective in a melody. Since the dominant triad contains the leading tone, it is often followed by the tonic. It is very strong to end a melody on $\hat{1}$. This is the most stable tone in any key. When you end a melody on $\hat{1}$ it is often preceded by $\hat{7}$ or $\hat{2}$, both notes of the dominant triad. A strong melodic ending consists of the final two notes $\hat{2}$ - $\hat{1}$ or $\hat{7}$ - $\hat{1}$. Figure 11.15 shows two strong endings for a melody using the notes of the dominant triad. a) outlines the dominant triad in C major (G B D) and ends on the tonic ($\hat{2}$ - $\hat{1}$). b) uses the root and 3rd of the dominant triad and ends on the tonic ($\hat{7}$ - $\hat{1}$).

Figure 11.15

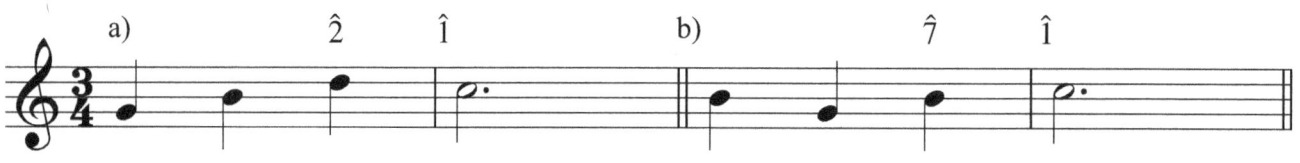

C major

❸ 1. Write a melody in F major using a combination of stepwise motion and skips outlining the tonic or dominant triad. Use the rhythm provided and end on a stable pitch ($\hat{1}$ or $\hat{3}$).

2. Write a melody in D major using a combination of stepwise motion and skips outlining the tonic or dominant triad. Use the rhythm provided and end on a stable pitch ($\hat{1}$ or $\hat{3}$).

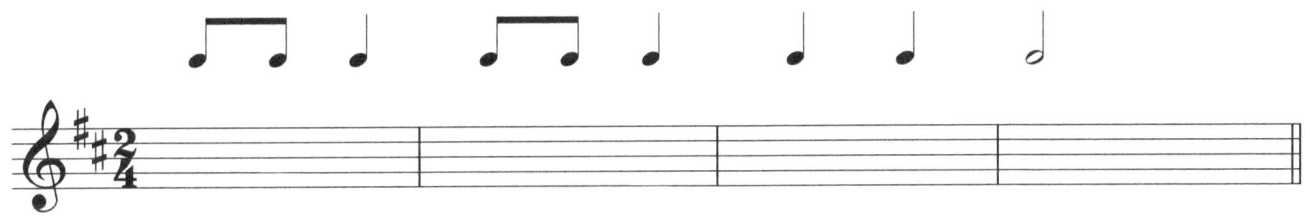

3. Write a melody in B♭ major using a combination of stepwise motion and skips outlining the tonic or dominant triad. Use the rhythm provided and end on a stable pitch ($\hat{1}$ or $\hat{3}$).

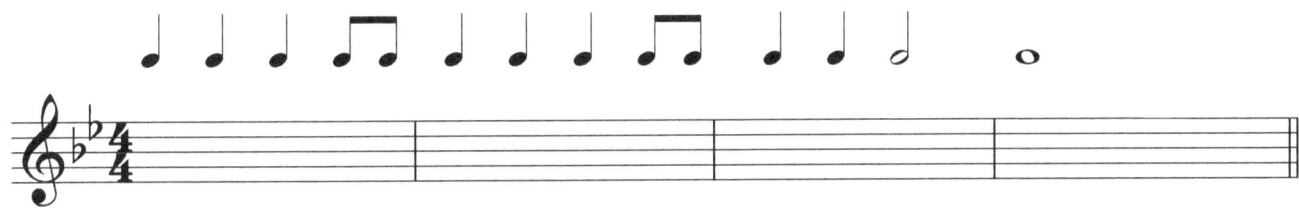

❸ 4. Write a melody in G major using a combination of stepwise motion and skips outlining the tonic or dominant triad. Use the rhythm provided and end on a stable pitch ($\hat{1}$ or $\hat{3}$).

5. Write a melody in C major using a combination of stepwise motion and skips outlining the tonic or dominant triad. Use the rhythm provided and end on a stable pitch ($\hat{1}$ or $\hat{3}$).

12

Music Analysis

❶ All of the concepts we have studied in theory can be put to good use when we look at a piece of
❷ music. *Music analysis* is studying a composition and figuring out its features. In this lesson,
❸ we are going to look at music and answer questions using the information we have learned.

1. Answer the questions relating to the following melodies.

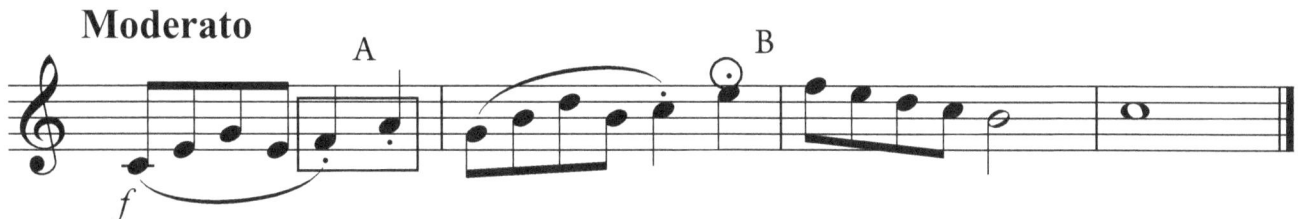

a. Add the correct time signature directly on the music.

b. Name the key of this piece._____

c. Name the interval number at A._____

d. Find and circle a C major triad. Label it "C."

e. Find and circle a G major triad. Label it "G."

f. Define *Moderato*._____

g. Name and define the sign at letter B._____

h. Find a motive and draw a square around each time it occurs.

i. How many slurs are in this piece? _____

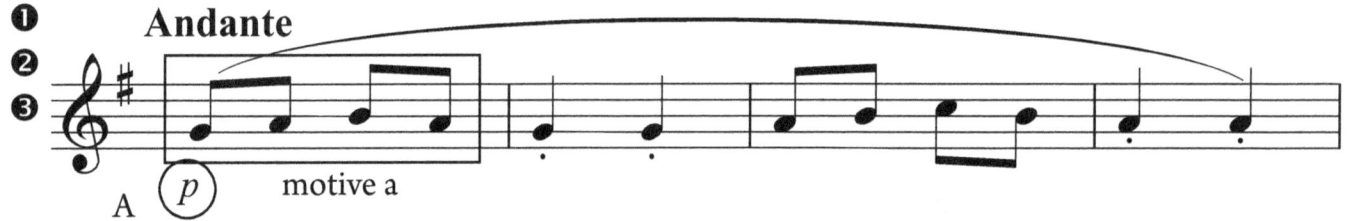
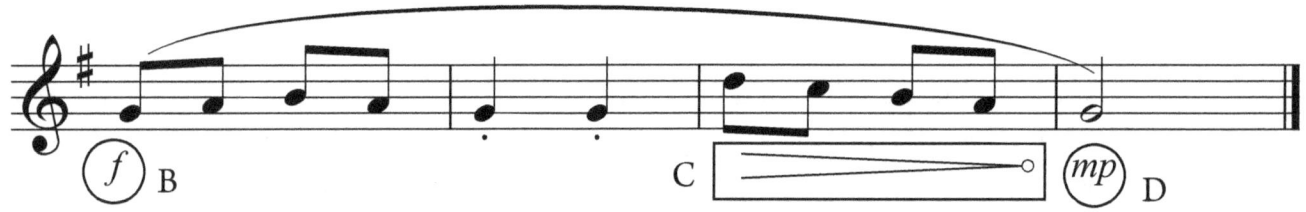

a. Add the correct time signature directly on the music.

b. Name the key of this piece._____

c. Circle each time motive "a" appears in this piece.

d. How many phrases are in this piece? _____.

e. On which scale degree does phrase two end?_____

f. Define **Andante**._____

g. Name and define the sign at letter A._____

h. Name and define the sign at letter B._____

i. Name and define the sign at letter C. _____

j. Name and define the sign at letter D._____

Bagatelle

Anton Diabelli
(1781 - 1858)

Allegro

a. What is the title of this piece? _____

b. Who is the composer? _____

c. Name the key of this piece. _____

d. Add the time signature directly on the music.

e. How many phrases are in this piece? _____.

f. On which scale degree does the melody of this piece begin? _____

g. Define *Allegro*. _____

h. Name the interval number at A. _____

i. Name the interval number at B. _____

j. This piece is played:

  ❏ loud   ❏ soft

Music Analysis

❷ 1. Answer questions relating to the following musical example.
❸

Allegro

A *ff* B

a. Add the correct time signature directly on the music.

b. Name the key of this piece._____

c. Circle a complete F major scale in this piece.

d. Draw a phrase mark over the phrase.

e. On which scale degree does this phrase end?_____

f. Is this a stable degree? _____

g. Define *Allegro*._____

h. Explain the sign at letter A._____

i. Explain the sign at letter B._____

j. Label all the leading tones LT.

❷
❸ **Presto**

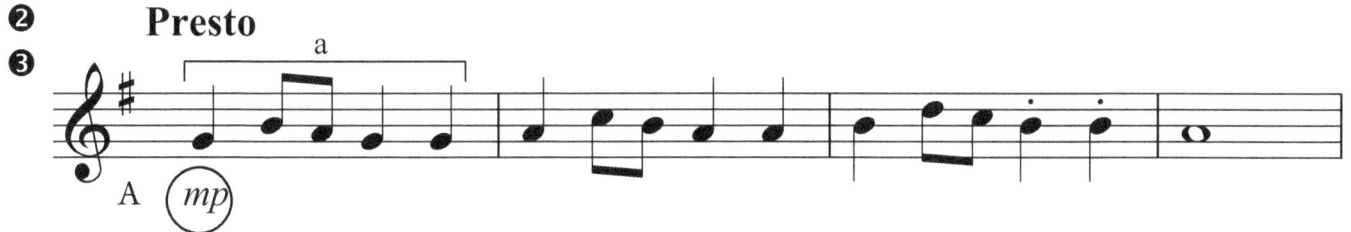

a. Add the correct time signature directly on the music.

b. Name the key of this piece._____

c. Circle each time motive "a" appears in this piece.

d. There are two phrases. Draw a phrase mark over each phrase.

e. On which scale degree does this phrase one end?_____

f. Is this a stable degree? _____

g. Define **Presto**._____

h. Explain the sign at letter A._____

i. Explain the sign at letter B._____

j. Name and define the sign at letter C. _____

Allegro in C

Alexander Reinagle
(1756 - 1809)

Molto allegro

a. Give the title of this piece. _____

b. Add the correct time signature directly on the music.

c. Name the key of this piece. _____

d. Name the composer of this piece. _____

e. When did he live? _____

f. There are two phrases. Draw a phrase mark over each phrase.

g. On which scale degree does phrase two end? _____

h. Is this a stable degree? _____

i. Define *Molto allegro*. _____

j. Name and define the sign at A. _____

k. Name the interval at B. _____

Music Analysis

❸ Form in Melody

The overall plan or structure of a piece of music is known as form. We label music with letters to distinguish the differences within a composition.

Let's examine the two phrase melody in Figure 12.1. This melody is in the key of D major and begins on the stable scale degree $\hat{3}$ (F♯). The first phrase ends on the unstable degree $\hat{2}$ (E). The second phrase begins like the first and continues until the end where the last bar is slightly different, ending on the stable scale degree $\hat{1}$ (D).

We can label each phrase with a letter to indicate the form. The first phrase is labeled 'a.' The second phrase being the same, except for the ending, is labeled 'a¹.' This shows that the phrases are related, but there is a slight variation. If the phrases were exactly the same, they would be labeled with two 'a's. It should be noted that each phrase is four measures long. This is a common length for a phrase.

These two phrases together form a section called a parallel period. A parallel period is formed when the two phrases are similar.

Figure 12.1

Music Analysis

❸ Figure 12.2 contains a melody that is made up of two distinctly different phrases. Each phrase begins with a quarter note upbeat. This, along with the rhythm, which is the same between the two phrases, is a unifying feature. However, the phrases are still very different. The first phrase contains a melody that ascends, and the second phrase contains a melody that descends. They work well together, but are not the same. To show this difference, the first phrase is labeled '**a**' and the second phrase is labeled '**b**.'

These two phrases together form a section called a ***contrasting period***. A contrasting period occurs when the two phrases of a period are different or contrasting.

Figure 12.2

Scottish Air

F major

1. For the following melodies: name the key, mark the phrases, and label them with letters (a, a^1, b) indicating their form.

Welsh Air

key:

Irish Air

key:

American Folk Tune

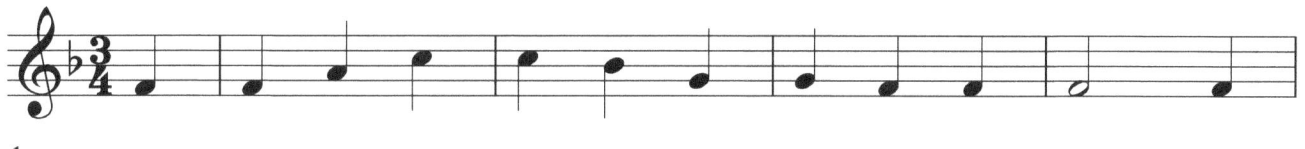

key:

Carol based on Chant
"O Come, O Come Emmanuel"

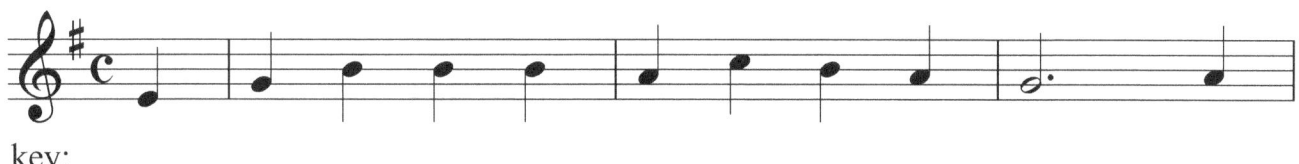

key:

© San Marco Publications 2023   154   Music Analysis

Allegro

Alexander Reinagle
(1756 - 1809)

a. Add the correct time signature directly on the music.

b. Name the key of this piece._____

c. Name the composer of this piece. _____

d. Draw a phrase mark over each phrase.

e. Label the phrases according to the form (a, a¹, b)

f. These two phrases form a: ☐ contrasting period   ☐ parallel period

g. Does the second phrase end on a stable or unstable degree? _____

h. Define *Allegro*._____

i. How are measure 1 and 2 similar to 5 and 6? _____

j. Locate and circle a half step in this piece.

Carefree

Daniel Gottlob Turk
(1756 - 1813)

a. Add the correct time signature directly on the music.

b. Name the key of this piece._____

c. Name the composer of this piece. _____

d. Draw a phrase mark over each phrase.

e. Label the phrases according to the form (a, a¹, b)

f. These two phrases form a: ❏ contrasting period   ❏ parallel period

g. Does the second phrase end on a stable or unstable degree? _____

h. Define **Moderato**._____

i. Find and circle one accidental in this piece.

j. Name the interval at letter A. _____

k. Name the interval at letter B. _____

❸

Bagatelle

Anton Diabelli

a. Add the correct time signature directly on the music.

b. Name the key of this piece._____

c. Name the composer of this piece. _____

d. Draw a phrase mark over each phrase.

e. Label the phrases according to the form (a, a¹, b)

f. Does the second phrase end on a stable or unstable degree? _____

g. Find and circle one dominant triad in this piece.

h. Name the interval at letter A. _____

i. Name the interval at letter B. _____

j. Explain the sign at letter C. _____

k. On what measure does this piece begin? _____

© San Marco Publications 2023

157

Music Analysis

History Level 1

The Orchestra

An *orchestra* is a performing group made up of many different musical instruments. Orchestra is a Greek word that originally referred to the area directly in front of a stage. When you attend an orchestral performance, you will see the orchestra playing in that exact place.

The orchestra as we know it today began with Italian opera around the year 1600. Opera was a sung play composed for singers and accompanied by a group of musicians that sat in front of the stage. Early orchestras performed short pieces called *overtures* before the opera started.

The music produced by these groups became so popular that composers started to write large pieces exclusively for them called *symphonies*. This is the reason orchestras are often called 'symphony orchestras.'

By the middle of the 19th century, these orchestras developed a standard group of instruments that has remained to the present day. The modern orchestra contains four main instrument sections:

- **strings** (violin, viola, cello, bass)
- **woodwinds** (flute, clarinet, oboe, bassoon, piccolo, English horn)
- **brass** (trumpet, trombone, tuba, French horn)
- **percussion** (timpani, drums, triangle, gong, cymbals, xylophone, piano, tambourine, +)

To keep the orchestra together, and help them play with the correct rhythm and expression, a *conductor* stands in front of them and directs them using hand gestures.

Camille Saint-Saens (1835 - 1921) Romantic Era

Camille Saint-Saens was born October 9, 1835, in Paris, France. He began studying piano at age two and a half and wrote his first piano piece when he was three. He started performing when he was a young boy and made his Paris recital debut at the age of ten.

Saint-Saens was not just brilliant at music. He also excelled at mathematics and science. He studied music at the Paris Conservatoire and won many prizes there. He became a follower of the great virtuoso pianist, organist, and composer, Franz Liszt.

Saint-Saens composed almost every kind of musical work including symphonies, concertos, and operas. One of his compositions, the Carnival of the Animals, was written as a sort of joke, but it is now his most famous work. He also wrote, books, poetry, and plays.

Saint-Saens influenced other well know French composers, especially Maurice Ravel and Gabriel Fauré.

Saint-Saens is considered a Romantic composer. The Romantic era was a period in time from approximately 1820 to 1910. There are many great composers from this era including:

- Frédéric Chopin
- Robert Schumann
- Felix Mendelssohn
- Johannes Brahms
- Pyotr Tchaikovsky
- Franz Liszt
- Hector Berlioz

The Carnival of the Animals

One of Saint-Saens most well-known compositions is ***The Carnival of the Animals***. It is written for two pianos and orchestra. He had fun describing some of his friends as animals. This piece is known throughout the world for its musical portrayal of animals. Some of the animals he portrays in music include the lion, hens and roosters, the turtle, the elephant, the kangaroo, the cuckoo, and the swan. There are also sections describing an aquarium, an aviary, fossils, people with long ears (donkeys), and a pianist. We will discuss the pieces titled: *Kangaroos, Aquarium,* and *The Swan*. The Carnival of the Animals is *descriptive* or **program music**. Program music is designed to portray a picture, object or story with sound.

Kangaroos

Saint-Saens wrote *Kangaroos* for two pianos. The main melody features hopping 5ths in the theme. When they go up, the tempo gradually speeds up, and the dynamics get louder. When the fifths go down, the tempo gradually slows down, and the dynamics get quieter.

Aquarium

Aquarium is written for two pianos, strings, flute and glass harmonica. In this piece, the composer describes water by trickling runs on the two pianos. The swimming of the fish is portrayed by a smooth melody in the strings and flute. The sound of water droplets was written for the **glass harmonica**, an instrument from the 19th century. It produces a sound much like when you run your fingers around the top of a water glass. It is usually played on the glockenspiel today because glass harmonicas are difficult to find.

The Swan

The Swan is the most famous section of The Carnival of the Animals. It is written for two pianos and cello. A beautiful melody is played by the cello while the pianos play rippling notes and broken chords that describe the swans feet gliding under the water.

Search the internet and listen to a performance of Carnival of the Animals.

Camille Saint Saens Crossword

Complete the crossword below.

Word List

Swan
Two
Turtle
Romantic
Elephant
Orchestra
Kangaroo
France
Cello
Donkey
Hens
Glass Harmonica
Two Pianos

Across

3. Chickens
4. Long eared animal
6. Where Saint Saens was born
7. Carnival of the Animals is written for 2 pianos and _____
12. Era in which Saint Saens composed
13. Number of pianos in Carnival of the Animals

Down

1. The Swan is written for _____
2. Rare instrument used in Aquarium
5. Jumping Australian animal
8. Large African animal with trunk
9. Instruments featured in Kangaroos
10. Slow moving animal with shell
11. Gliding water bird

❶ Choose the correct answer.
❷
❸

a. An orchestra is led by the:	☐	Pitcher	☐	Conductor
	☐	President	☐	Mayor

b. This instrument is not part of the string section	☐	Violin	☐	Cello
	☐	Viola	☐	Maracas

c. This instrument is not part of the woodwind section:	☐	Flute	☐	Oboe
	☐	Clarinet	☐	French Horn

d. Camille Saint-Saens was born in:	☐	Canada	☐	France
	☐	China	☐	Russia

e. Saint-Saens wrote his first piano piece when he was:	☐	3	☐	2
	☐	10	☐	32

f. Carnival of the Animals is written for orchestra and:	☐	Flute	☐	2 pianos
	☐	3 banjos	☐	Trumpet

g. This animal is not in Carnival of the Animals:	☐	Kangaroo	☐	Elephant
	☐	Wolf	☐	Lion

h. Aquarium is written for 2 pianos, strings, flute, and:	☐	Cello	☐	Horn
	☐	Guitar	☐	Glass Harmonica

i. The Swan is written for 2 pianos and:	☐	Flute	☐	Cello
	☐	Lute	☐	Harp

j. Carnival of the Animals is:	☐	Rock Music	☐	Program Music
	☐	Jazz Music	☐	Opera

History

Sergei Prokofiev (1891 - 1953) Modern Era

Russian composer and pianist **Sergei Prokofiev** was born in 1891 in a small village in Ukraine. From a young age, he had a gift for music. Prokofiev began studying piano with his mother when he was three. At five, he wrote his first composition, and at nine, he wrote his first opera. He studied music at the St Petersburg Conservatory from 1904 to 1914.

Prokofiev was a gifted pianist and often performed his works in concert.

Prokofiev's music was more innovative and different sounding than anything ever heard before. It used unusual harmonies and intense rhythms.

After the Russian revolution, Prokofiev moved to America. However, American audiences did not fully appreciate his music. In 1923 he settled in Paris where he was very successful, and his music was well received. In 1936 Prokofiev returned to Russia, where he spent the last 19 years of his life. During this period, he wrote some of his best works.

Prokofiev loved to use music to tell a story. One of his most famous compositions that tells a story is **Peter and the Wolf,** which he composed for Russia's Central Children's Theatre. In addition to symphonies, Prokofiev wrote ballets, operas, concertos, piano pieces, movie scores and more.

Peter and the Wolf

Prokofiev wrote Peter and the Wolf in 1936 for narrator and orchestra. It is a story in music that includes both people and animals.
Like Saint-Saens Carnival of the Animals, this is program music. Here, along with a narrator, the music tells a story.

Each character in the story has a particular instrument and a musical theme:

    Peter: string instruments (including violin, viola, cello, and bass)
    Bird: flute
    Cat: clarinet
    Duck: oboe
    Grandfather: bassoon
    Hunters: woodwind theme, with gunshots on timpani and bass drum
    Wolf: French horns

Peter, a young boy, lives with his grandfather near a forest. One day, Peter goes out, leaving the garden gate open, and the duck that lives in the yard gets out and goes swimming in a nearby pond. The duck starts arguing with a little bird. Peter's pet cat sneaks up on them quietly, and the bird flies to safety in a tall tree while the duck swims to the middle of the pond.

Peter's grandfather is angry at him for being in the forest alone. What if a wolf was in the forest? Peter says: "Boys like me are not afraid of wolves." His grandfather takes him back into the house. Afterword, "a big, grey wolf" does come out of the forest. The cat climbs into a tree, but the duck, who has jumped out of the pond, is caught and swallowed by the wolf.

Peter grabs a rope and scampers over the garden wall into the tree. He tells the bird to fly around the wolf's head and distract it. Then he catches the wolf by the tail.

Hunters come out of the forest and want to shoot the wolf, but Peter convinces them to take the wolf to a zoo. The narrator completes the story by saying: "If you listen very carefully, you'll hear the duck quacking inside the wolf's belly because the wolf in his hurry had swallowed her alive."

Search the internet and listen to a performance of Peter and the Wolf.

Sergei Prokofiev Word Search

```
S T R I N G S D Q O
R E F I V E V C D R
P R O G R A M L U C
J U T Y U I O P C H
H S X C W O L F K E
G S A M O D E R N S
F I B A S S O O N T
D A G O A D C N M R
B I R D G H A E R A
O B O E A T T B E D
```

Word List

Russia
wolf
oboe
five
duck
bassoon
Modern
program
cat
orchestra
bird
strings

1. Where was Prokofiev born? _____

2. At what age did Prokofiev begin composing? _____

3. In what musical era did he compose? _____

4. Peter and the Wolf is written for narrator and _____

5. What type of music is Peter and the Wolf? _____

6. Name 4 animals in Peter and the Wolf. _____ _____ _____ _____

7. What instruments are used to portray Peter? _____

8. What instrument is used to portray the grandfather? _____

9. What instument is used to portray the duck? _____

165

History

History Level 2

❷❸ Wolfgang Amadeus Mozart (1756 - 1791) Classical Era

Wolfgang Amadeus Mozart composed music in the ***classical era.*** The classical era was a period in history between the years 1730 and 1820. Mozart was born in Salzburg, Austria, where his father and teacher Leopold was a violinist and composer. Wolfgang was a child prodigy. He composed his first piece of music at age five, had his first piece published when he was seven, and he wrote his first opera when he was twelve. By the time Mozart was 6, he was a first-rate pianist and violinist. He and his sister Maria Anna (known as Nannerl) traveled all over Europe performing for royalty.

As an adult, Mozart moved to Vienna, to work as a pianist and composer. Mozart, no longer a child prodigy, was still a musical genius, but people no longer made a big fuss over him. At that time, musicians were treated like servants, but Mozart could never and would never think of himself as a servant.

Mozart was only 35 when he died. During his short life, he composed in all different musical forms, including operas, symphonies, concertos, masses, and chamber music. Today, he is still considered one of the greatest composers of all time!

Catalogue Numbers for Mozart Compositions

Many composers assigned numbers to their compositions. This helped to identify them. If a composer wrote four Sonatas in C major, it was easier to identify them if they were numbered. Mozart, however, never numbered his works.

In 1862, a Viennese botanist and teacher named Ludwig von Köchel, published a catalogue of Mozart's compositions in chronological order. He assigned Köchel (K) numbers to each of Mozarts works according to the date of composition. For example, the Horn Concerto we are going to study is labeled K495. It is approximately the 495th piece of music that Mozart composed.

Horn Concerto No. 4 in E flat Major, K 495

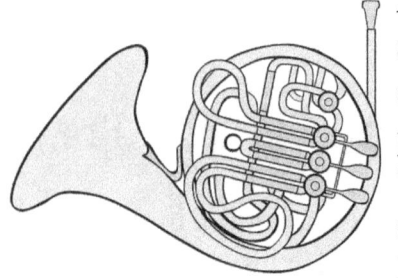

A *concerto* is a musical composition which features a single solo instrumentalist with an orchestral accompaniment. It shows off the skills of the soloist and the musical potential of the instrument being played.

This concerto is for french horn and orchestra. It was written my Mozart in 1786 for his friend, French horn player, Joseph Leutgeb.

Mozart wrote it in four colors of ink, black, red, blue, and green as a joke for his friend Joseph. Mozart had a great sense of humor.

This concerto has four sections called *movements*.

The last movement is a *Rondo*. It features a melody which is a hunting theme, which returns over and over throughout the piece. Rondos always have a section that returns many times over. Between this section are new sections consisting of different melodies or themes and musical ideas. After each new idea the original theme returns. Find and listen to a recording of this Rondo on the internet.

Twelve Variations on "Ah vous dirai-je, Maman"

Twelve Variations on "Ah vous dirai-je, Maman" K. 265, is a piano composition by Mozart, composed when he was about 25 years old (1781 or 1782). In music, variations are pieces that are based on a tune, known as the theme. This form is often called Theme and Variations. This piece consists of twelve variations on the French folk song "Ah! vous dirai-je, Maman". This well-known melody first appeared in 1761, and has been used for many children's songs, such as "Twinkle Twinkle Little Star," "Baa, Baa, Black Sheep," and the "Alphabet Song."

Mozart's Variations are composed for solo piano and consist of 13 sections; the first section is the theme, the other sections are Variations 1 to 12.

The variations were first published in Vienna in 1785.

❷ Choose the correct answer.
❸

a. Mozart was born in:	☐	France	☐	Germany
	☐	Poland	☐	Austria
b. Mozart's first teacher was:	☐	His father	☐	His mother
	☐	His sister	☐	Haydn
c. What era did Mozart live?	☐	modern	☐	classical
	☐	romantic	☐	baroque
d. What is the solo instrument in Mozart's Horn concerto?	☐	flute	☐	piano
	☐	french horn	☐	oboe
e. Mozart's Horn Concerto in E♭ has 4 sections called:	☐	groups	☐	movements
	☐	pieces	☐	dances
f. The last movement of Mozart's Horn Concerto in E♭ is a:	☐	rondo	☐	waltz
	☐	sonata	☐	minuet
g. Mozart's Variations on Ah vous dirai-je, Maman are written for:	☐	guitar	☐	orchestra
	☐	piano	☐	horn
h. How many variations did Mozart write on Ah vous dirai-je Maman?	☐	12	☐	9
	☐	6	☐	32
i. The melody upon which variations are based is called the:	☐	subject	☐	phrase
	☐	tune	☐	theme
j. The melody of these variations has been used for these childrens songs:	☐	Twinkle Twinkle	☐	Baa Baa Black Sheep
	☐	Alphabet Song	☐	Mary Had a Little Lamb

History

History Level 3

❸ Johann Sebastian Bach (1685 - 1750) Baroque Era

Johann Sebastian Bach was born in Eisenach, Germany where his father, a musician, taught him to play violin and harpsichord. Many of Bach's relatives were also musicians. His older brother, Johann Christoph Bach taught him to play the organ.

In 1707, Bach married his cousin Maria Barbara Bach. They had seven children. Maria died, and Bach married Anna Magdalena Wilcke in 1721. They had 13 more children. In total, Bach had 20 children. Some of Bach's sons became well-known composers. Carl Phillip Emmanuel Bach and Johann Christian Bach are two of them.

One of Bach's first serious jobs was working for a duke. After that, he was hired to compose for a prince. His final job was the director of music at St. Thomas Church and School in Leipzig, Germany. Here he was cantor (music teacher), organist, and music composer. He was very busy teaching, conducting, performing, and writing music. While in Leipzig he conducted a small group of local musicians who sometimes played at coffee houses.

Bach wrote a lot of music. His works fill many large volumes and contain, choral music, concertos, orchestra and chamber music and organ and keyboard music. Some of Bachs most famous compositions are the Brandenburg Concertos and The Well Tempered Clavier, written as teaching pieces for his students. He also wrote many great works for organ including the famous Toccata and Fugue in D minor.

Bach is considered one of the greatest musicians and composers that ever lived. However, during his life, he was hardly known. About 100 years after his death another composer named Felix Mendelssohn brought attention to his music, and the world finally realized Bach's greatness.

Bach composed during the Baroque era, which was between the years 1600 and 1750. Baroque music has tuneful melodies and can be very dramatic. The melodies are often very elaborate and decorated with trills and ornaments. Bach died in 1750.

❸ The Anna Magdalena Bach Notebook

The *Anna Magdalena Bach Notebook* refers to two books that composer Johann Sebastian Bach gave to his second wife, Anna Magdalena on her birthday. Bach wanted Anna Magdalena to copy music of her choosing into the books. They contain keyboard music and a few pieces for voice.

One book is dated 1722, and the other is dated 1725. The better-known book is the one from 1725. It is richly decorated with gold leaf and is a beautiful book.

Anna Magdalena was a musician and singer. Most of the pieces in the book are in Anna Magdalena's handwriting, and the true identity of many of the original composers in the book is not known. There seems to be writing in the book by members of Bach's family including Carl Phillip Emmanuel Bach, and Johann Christian Bach, two of his sons. The first two pieces in the book were copied by J. S. Bach himself.

The books contain several dances, arias, chorales and other pieces of music by different composers. These composers were probably Carl Philip Emmanuel Bach, Christian Petzold, François Couperin, and other musician friends of the Bach family.

Most of these pieces were written for musical enjoyment, but also as teaching pieces for younger members of the Bach family.

Anna Magdalena loved to have musical gatherings at the Bach house where visitors were encouraged to perform and compose new pieces which were copied into the notebook.

The Harpischord

The **harpsichord,** a keyboard instrument, is an early relative of the piano. It looks a little like a grand piano but sounds much different.
The harpsichord has small hooks called quills that pluck the string when a player presses a key on the keyboard. Because of this, it is very challenging to make dynamic changes when playing the harpsichord. Since the strings are plucked, the keyboard is not touch sensitive, and the player does not have control over the volume of each note.
The pieces in the Anna Magdalena Notebook were written for a harpsichord or a similar keyboard instrument.

❸ The Baroque Dance

A *Baroque dance* is an instrumental dance composed during the Baroque era (1600 - 1750). Dance music was very popular in the Baroque era, and composers were often asked to write dances for parties and functions.

The Anna Magdalena Notebook contains some of these Baroque dances written for keyboard. One of the most common dances found in this notebook is the *minuet*. A minuet is a dance for two people in 3/4 time that originated in France. It may be spelled differently in different countries. In Italy, it was called the *minuetto* and in France the *menuet*. Eventually, minuets were written for non-dancing purposes and became a musical form used for keyboard pieces and movements of symphonies. Minuets can also be found in operas, ballets, and plays.

One of the most famous minuets ever written, the *Minuet in G Major*, is in the Anna Magdalena Notebook. We are not exactly sure who wrote it, but credit is given to the composer Christian Petzold. The melody from this minuet has been used in pop songs and movie themes. The example below contains the opening eight measures of this famous minuet. Play it and see if you recognize it.

Another common dance from the Baroque era is the ***gavotte***. The gavotte is a folk dance from France. The music for a gavotte has a four beat feel and is moderately fast. It usually starts with upbeats (or an anacrusis) on beats three and four. Gavottes written in the Baroque period were not written for dancing but as musical pieces to listen to and enjoy.

Composers began writing **Suites**, which were larger compositions consisting of six or seven short dance-based pieces. The gavotte was often one of these pieces. The best-known examples of the gavotte are found in the suites written by J.S.Bach.

The following musical excerpt is the beginning of the Gavotte from J.S. Bach's French Suite in G major, BWV 816. BWV is a catalog number given to Bach's compositions to identify them. This gavotte is the fourth dance in the suite, and it is written for harpsichord.

This dance begins with two quarter note upbeats. This is a characteristic of a gavotte. The time signature ₵ is an abbreviation for 2/2 time. The top number tells us that there are two beats in each measure and the bottom number tells us that the half note receives one beat.

In this piece, the stems in the treble clef are placed in two directions. This indicates that the right hand is playing two different melodies. One melody has the stems going up, and one melody has the stems going down. The lower melody in the treble clef in mm.3-4 has three quarter rests. Here, the bottom voice is resting. The bass clef has its own melody. Music from the Baroque period is often based on 2, 3, 4, or more melodies that all work together to create a composition. This is called ***counterpoint***.

Search the internet for a recording of this Gavotte. Try to find a performance using the harpsichord to hear how it sounds on this instrument.

Another popular dance in the Baroque suite is the *gigue*. Gigue is the French word for a lively dance in triple time. In Italian, it is called "*giga*," and in English, it is "*jig*." The gigue is often seen in the Baroque dance suite as the last piece or movement.

Gigues use time signatures like 6/8, 9/8, or 12/16. Melodies are made up of rapidly moving groups of three eighth or three sixteenth notes. Most gigues are divided into four measure phrases and are written in counterpoint, using 2, 3, or more melodies that work together.

The following excerpt is the Gigue from French Suite in G Major, BWV 816, by J.S. Bach. This piece is written for harpsichord. The gigue begins with one melody in the treble clef. A second melody starts at the end of measure 3 in the treble clef. Here, the stems go in the opposite direction to show the two different melodies. A third melody is added at the end of measure 6, in the left hand. All three of these lines work together to create a masterful piece of music.

History

❸ Answer the following questions.

a) What musical era did J.S. Bach live? _____

b) When did this era occur? _____

c) In what country was he born? _____

d) What is the Anna Magdalena Notebook? _____

e) Name two composers whose music is in the Anna Magdalena Notebook.

    1) _____

    2) _____

f) Name three types of pieces found the the Anna Magdalena Notebook.

    1) _____ 2) _____ 3) _____

g) What instrument are these pieces written for? _____

h) What type of instrument is this? _____

i) In what country did the minuet originate? _____

j) What is the time signature of a minuet? _____

k) In what country did the gavotte originate? _____

l) Does the gavotte begin with an anacrusis? _____

m) What is a suitable Italian term for the tempo of a gigue? _____

n) The notes of a gigue usually occur in groups of _____

o) Where does the gigue usually occur in the Baroque dance suite? _____

Music Terms and Signs

Terms

accent — a stressed note

allegretto — fairly fast, a little slower than allegro

allegro — fast

andante — moderately slow, at a walking pace

a tempo — return to the original tempo

cantabile — in a singing style

crescendo, cresc. — becoming louder

da capo, D.C. — from the beginning

D.C. al fine — repeat from the beginning and end at *Fine*

dal segno, D.S. — from the sign

decrescendo, decresc. — becoming softer

diminuendo, dim. — becoming softer

dolce — sweetly, gentle

fine — the end

forte, f — loud

fortissimo, ff — very loud

grazioso — gracefully

legato	smooth
lento	slow
maestoso	majestically
marcato	play marked or stressed
mezzo forte, mf	moderately loud
mezzo piano, mp	moderately soft
moderato	at a moderate tempo
molto	much, very
ottava, 8va	the interval of an octave
pianissimo, pp	very soft
piano, p	soft
poco	little
presto	very fast
rallentando, rall.	slowing down
ritardando, rit.	slowing down gradually
staccato	play short and detached
tempo	speed at which music is performed

Signs

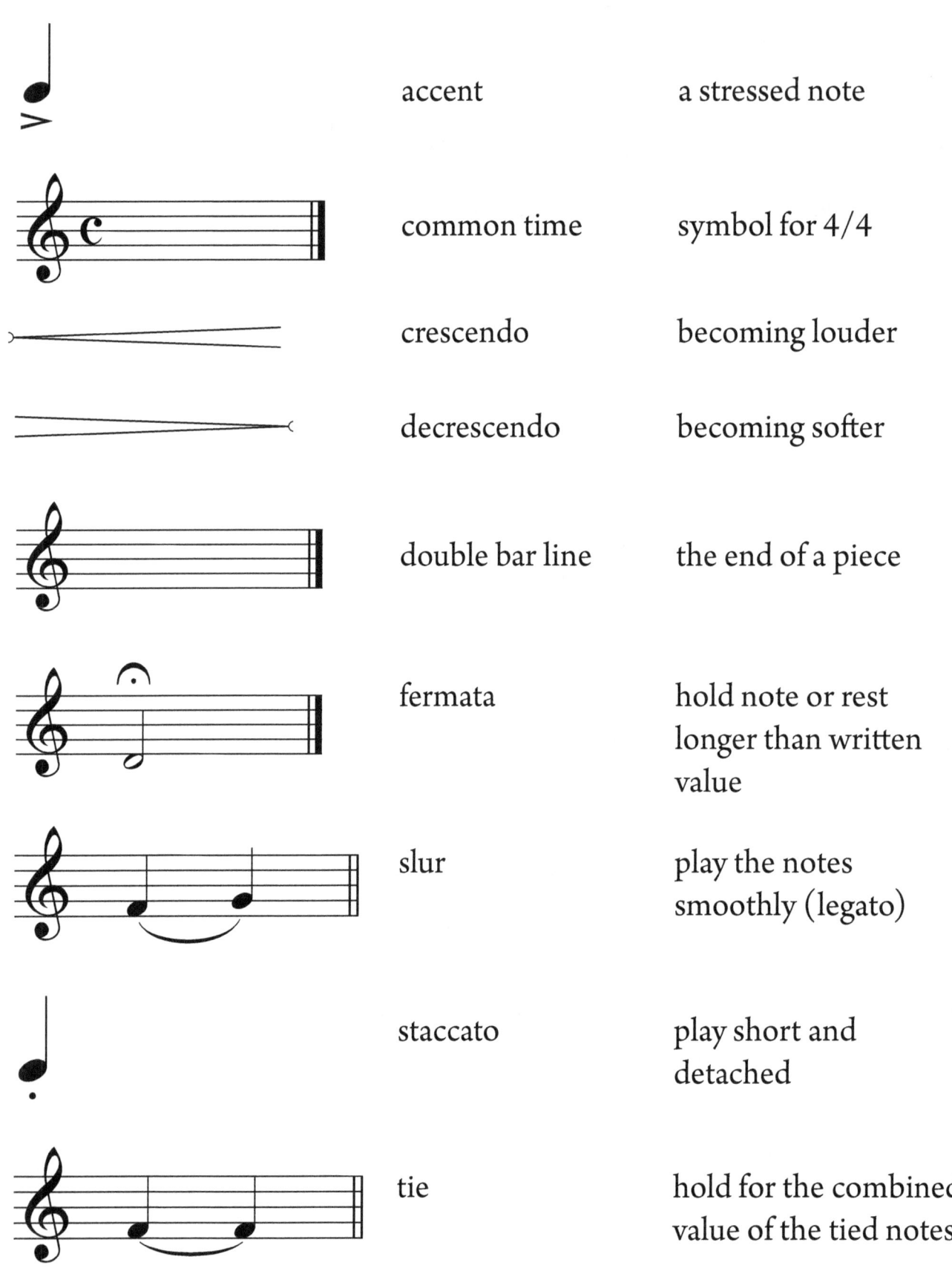

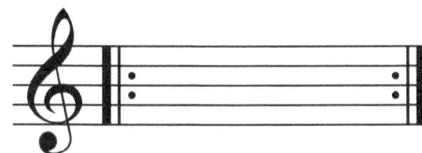 **repeat marks** - at the second sign go back to the first sign and repeat the music from there. The first sign is left out if the music is repeated from the beginning.

 **tenuto mark** - when placed over or under a note, hold it for its full value.

 **pedal symbol** - press/release the right pedal.

 **dal segno, D.S.** - from the sign.

8va - play one octave higher than written pitch.

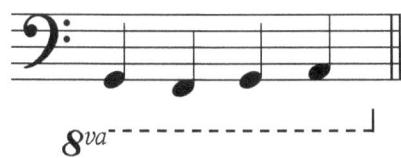 **8va** - play one octave lower than written pitch.

www.ingramcontent.com/pod-product-compliance
Lightning Source LLC
Chambersburg PA
CBHW081617100526
44590CB00021B/3481